What's that over there?

M1 + A1

Copyright © White Line Press 1993

ISBN 0 948205 04 0

First published 1993 by
White Line Press
60 Bradford Road, Stanningley, Leeds LS28 6EF

Design: Chris Oxlade and Krystyna Hewitt
Layout: Phil Gardner and Chris Oxlade

Illustrations: Steve Beaumont and Chris Oxlade

Cover photographs: Noel Whittall

Printed and bound in Great Britain

This book is copyright under the Berne Convention. All rights are reserved. Apart from any fair dealing for the purposes of private study, research, criticism or review, as permitted under the Copyright, Designs and Patents Act 1988, no part of this publication may be reproduced, stored in a retrieval system, or transmitted in any form or by any means, electronic, electrical, chemical, mechanical, optical, photocopying, recording or otherwise, without the prior written permission of the copyright owner. Enquiries should be addressed to the Publisher.

Acknowledgements

Special thanks are due to Rosita and Matthew Whittall for patient help with research and driving, and to Andrew Shackleton for his valuable work in checking locations, road junctions and distances (any errors remaining are ours, not his).

Books in this series

What's that over there? covers the following major routes:

M1 + A1

In course of preparation:
M5 + M6
M4 + M40
M25 and adjoining short motorways

What's that over there?

M1 + A1

Noel Whittall
Chris Oxlade

Winter 1995

Update and errata M1 + A1

p 19 Many of the Daventry radio masts removed

p 31 Sutton Scarsdale hall is *west*

p 40 Woolley Colliery now demolished

p 66 Brampton Hotel now demolished

p 91 Temple of Victory restored!

pp 91-94 The A1 upgraded to motorway; follows route of old A1, but now difficult to spot all the Devil's Arrows from a car

WHITE LINE PRESS

Preface

How often have you said "what's that over there?" during a trip along a motorway? Never? Don't believe you!

Motorway journeys can be very boring indeed, but if you have just some idea of the features in the landscape through which you are being driven, the time can pass far more pleasantly.

This book points out some of the things which have caught our eyes as we have motored around the country. We make no claim to have covered everything that you will see, nor have we attempted to provide more than the most basic details. The only rules we have applied are that in average weather conditions you should have a fair chance of spotting the features we mention, and that *we* found them interesting.

As soon as you start to assemble a book of this nature, you begin to discover just how much variety there is in the landscape, and how much it changes from season to season. A building which completely dominates the view when surrounded only by the stark branches of winter can disappear completely amongst the leaves of summer. If we have left out one of your favourites, please tell us about it and we will try to include it in the next edition.

Noel Whittall and Chris Oxlade
January 1993

Contents

M1: List of Features 6
M1 7
Special Feature: Time changes the landscape 49
A1: List of Features 56
A1 57

Finding the features

Although the M1 bends quite a lot in places, for simplicity we regard it as running north–south. Therefore anything which is on the left of the road as you travel from London to Leeds is described as being *west*, and everything on the right is *east*. The same principle applies to the A1.

The headings in capitals at the top of each page tell you which county the road is in when you are opposite the first feature (even pages) or last feature (odd pages). Usually the feature is in the same county — but not always!

On a reasonably clear day you should be able to see most of the features, and enough of them are so close to the road that there will always be *something* to see. Some features are more easily viewed from the opposite side of the road, so if you miss something on your outward trip, try to catch it on the way back. All the distances are approximate. Some landmarks, such as the mast at Emley Moor, will be visible for many miles, while others may only be glimpsed fleetingly through the trees.

Researching *What's that over there?* would have been very much more difficult without the Ordnance Survey's maps and Nikolaus Pevsner's *Buildings of Britain*. We are also grateful for the assistance we have received from British Coal, British Rail, the Department of Transport and many departments of tourism and water companies throughout the country.

Now sit back, make sure that the driver's eyes are on the road, and enjoy the scenery ...

Locating each feature

You can find the features by checking their positions on the plan which appears down the side of the left-hand pages. There is also a location guide beside each heading. This tells you how far you will be from the nearest junctions when you are level with the feature. For example:

Odhams Press Building ❸   1m N J5 ; 1.5m S J6 ; 0.5m W

The feature is number ❸ on the plan. It is about 1 mile north of Junction 5, 1.5 miles south of Junction 6, and half a mile to the west of the motorway. On the parts of the A1 where the junctions are not numbered, we use the road numbers at major junctions to help you fix the position.

M1: List of Features

RAF Museum, Hendon	8	St Peter, Whetstone	23	Ruins of Tankersley Hall	37
Railway	8	Narborough Hospital	23	Obelisk, Birdwell	38
Tower, St Joseph's	8	Mattel Toys warehouse	23	Wentworth Castle	38
London skyline	9	Leicester	24	BP Plastics factory	39
Gothic tower	10	British Shoe Corporation		Birthwaite Hall	39
Elstree Aerodrome	10	Distribution Centre	24	Woolley colliery	40
Odhams Press Building	10	Kirby Muxloe Castle	24	Bretton Hall	40
Chimneys, Leavesden		Old John Tower	25	Railway breathers,	
Hospital	11	Quarry Hill, Markfield	25	Woolley	41
Tower, Shenley Hospital	11	Beacon Hill	26	TV mast, Emley Moor	41
BP House	12	Loughborough	26	Viaduct, Calder Grove	41
Buncefield oil distribution		Site of Kegworth air		River Calder	42
centre	12	crash	26	Sandal Castle	42
Luton Hoo	12	East Midlands		St Peter and St Leonard,	
Stockwood Park	13	International Airport	26	Horbury	42
Luton	13	Ratcliffe-on-Soar Power		Holy Trinity, Ossett	43
Luton and Dunstable		Station	27	Chimney, Ossett	43
Hospital	13	Castle Donington Power		Wakefield skyline	44
Chiltern Hills	14	Station	27	Water tower, Dewsbury	45
Railway	14	River Trent	27	St Michael, East Ardsley	45
Cranfield	14	All Saints, Sawley	28	Rhubarb sheds	45
Milton Keynes	15	Church Wilne reservoir	28	Mining cottages	46
Great Ouse	15	Nottingham	28	Chloride Metals factory	46
Gayhurst House	15	Stanton Iron Works	29	Tower, St George's	
St James the Great,		All Saints, Strelley and		Hospital	46
Hanslope	16	Strelley Hall	29	Rail depot lights,	
Northampton	16	Watnall brickworks	30	Rothwell	46
St Benedict,		The Great Yellow Pipe		Skelton Grange Power	
Northampton	17	Factory	30	Station	47
Rothersthorpe locks	17	Hardwick Hall and		City of Leeds	47
Express Lifts tower	18	Hardwick Old Hall	30		
Hospitals, Northampton	18	Sutton Scarsdale Hall	31		
Bugbrooke Mill	18	Bolsover Castle	32	**Time changes the**	
Brockhall Hall	19	Markham mine	32	**landscape**	**49**
Daventry Radio Station	19	Barlborough Hall	32	*Earth hill forts*	*49*
Railway	20	Kiveton Park mine	33	*Long straight stretches*	
Roman road	20	Conical furnace,		*of road*	*49*
Grand Union Canal	20	Catcliffe	33	*Castles*	*49*
St Margaret, Crick	20	Steel works, Sheffield	33	*Stately homes*	*50*
Rugby Radio Station	21	Tinsley Viaduct	34	*Mills and factories*	*51*
Lilbourne All Saints,		Sheffield	34	*Airfields*	*51*
motte and bailey	21	Meadowhall shopping		*Canals and railways*	*52*
River Avon	21	centre, Tinsley	34	*Transmitting masts and*	
St Mary, Lutterworth	22	River Don	35	*aerials*	*52*
BOCM Silcock Ltd plant	22	Thundercliffe Grange	35	*Churches*	*52*
Chimney with aerials,		Keppel's Column	36	*Water towers*	*55*
Lutterworth	22	Hoober Stand	36		

M1

The M1 starts at Staples Corner on London's North Circular Road and finishes 194 miles later just south of Leeds city centre.

In Britain, motorway building did not start until the late 1950s, when the volume of traffic on the country's roads was increasing rapidly. The Italians beat us by more than thirty years in building their *autostrade*, the first of which opened in 1925. These were followed by German *Autobahnen* in the 1930s.

The British motorway programme started in 1958 with the opening of the eight-mile Preston by-pass. The first section of the M1 to be built was the 74-mile stretch from Bushey in Hertfordshire (at the current Junction 4) to Crick in Northamptonshire (now Junction 18), which was opened on 2 November 1959.

That first section of the M1 was built to take traffic from the heavily overloaded A5 and A6, and in many ways was an experiment to test the theories of Britain's motorway-building programme. This soon showed that the standard of construction was not high enough — extensive repairs had to be carried out in 1962.

In the 1960s Britain's motorway network continued to grow at the rate of about a mile per week.

The majority of the M1, from what is now Junction 2, to Stourton, just outside Leeds, was open by late 1968. Bits were added on the ends and the full length was completed in October 1972.

M1 — GREATER LONDON

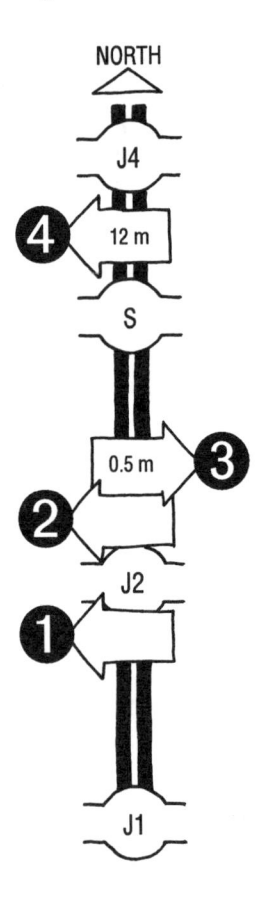

RAF Museum, Hendon ❶   2m N J1 ; 0.25m S J2 ; adjacent W

The roofs of the new buildings of the RAF Museum mark the edge of the old Hendon Aerodrome, a famous centre of British aviation since before the First World War. In the 20s and 30s, the Hendon air displays were the showcase for the RAF.

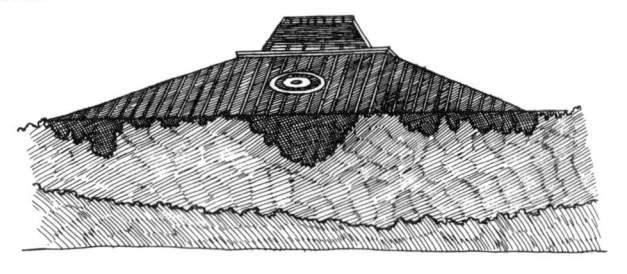

The last plane flew out of Hendon in 1957, and most of the airfield has since been developed for industrial use.

The RAF Museum was opened in 1972 and now houses the largest static collection of aircraft in England. We rate it well worth a visit. Open seven days a week.

Railway ❷   J2 northwards ; adjacent W

Alongside the road for a couple of miles is the main line to Leicester, Nottingham, Derby and Sheffield, and the commuter line to Luton and Bedford.

Tower, St Joseph's ❸   1m N J2 ; 3m S J4 ; 0.5m E

This is the campanile (isolated bell tower) which stands beside the chapel at St Joseph's Missionary College in Mill Hill. It is over a hundred feet high, and topped with a huge gilt-bronze statue of St Joseph.

GREATER LONDON — M1

The college was founded by Cardinal Vaughan and built between 1866 and 1871. Vaughan was an energetic and adventurous Roman Catholic churchman who was very keen on ecclesiastical education. To fund the college he went off round the world for two years begging for money. Much of his journeying was in Central America, and he did not have an easy time of it by any means. In Panama he escaped from gaol after being arrested for illegal preaching. He died in 1903 and is buried in the grounds of the college. Missionaries trained at St Joseph's are to be found throughout the world.

London skyline ④ Scratchwood Services to J4 ; 12m W

From the vicinity of the Scratchwood services, you can pick out the tops of the tallest buildings in London from among the endless mass of roofs. The thin Telecom Tower usually stands out clearly, but conditions have to be good to pick out some of the others, such as the pyramid-top of Canary Wharf, far away to the south-east in Docklands.

The Telecom Tower (620 ft; 190 m) was completed in 1964 as the Post Office Tower. Canary Wharf (800 ft; 245 m) is a 1990 newcomer.

JUNCTIONS

Hendon/ Edgware area

Junction 1
Staples Corner. A406 London North Circular Road

Junction 2
Access to the A41 and A1 to central London when travelling south only

Junction 3
At present there is no Junction 3!

Scratchwood services
The first services when travelling north.

Junction 4
Southbound access only to the A41 for Edgware

M1 — GREATER LONDON

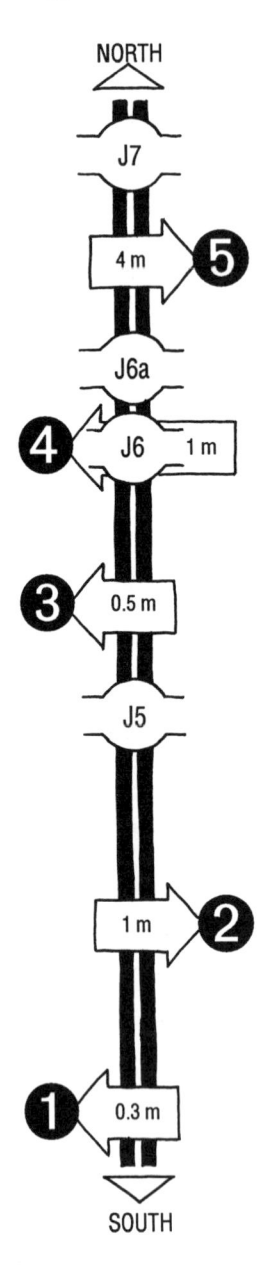

Gothic tower ❶   1.25m N J4 ; 3.75m S J5 ; 0.3m W

The tower rises from Caldecote Towers, a mid-Victorian extravaganza, now sadly in a state of disrepair. It was originally part of Rosary Priory High School, but now stands in the grounds of Immanuel College, opened in 1991.

Elstree Aerodrome ❷   2m N J4 ; 2m S J5 ; 1m E

Light aircraft are often a feature of the sky in this area, as they take off and land at Elstree Aerodrome, which is less than a mile to the east of the motorway.

Odhams Press Building ❸   1m N J5 ; 1.5m S J6 ; 0.5m W

The large windowless building surmounted with a small church-like clock-tower and spire is a printing works on the outskirts of Watford. It was originally built for Odhams, but then became part of the ill-fated Maxwell organisation. The

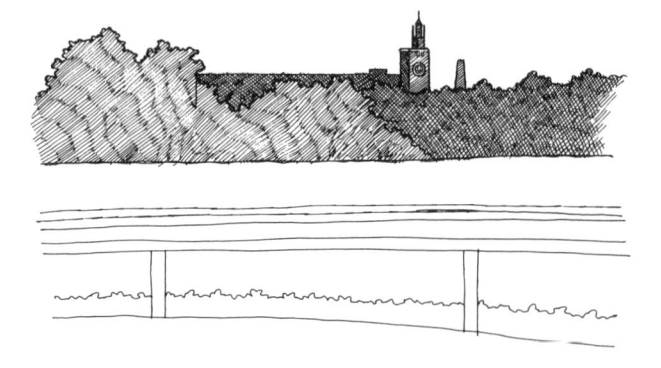

HERTFORDSHIRE — M1

colour sections of Mirror Group newspapers are printed here.

The building was considered very modern when it was built in 1937. The facade was designed by the architect Sir Owen Williams. During his distinguished career he worked on projects as varied as concrete ships and the Empire Stadium at Wembley. However, as you journey along the M1 you will encounter far more of his work, because he was the architect of much of the M1 motorway itself.

Chimneys, Leavesden Hospital ④ At J6 ; 1m W

The four parallel chimneys of the Horizon NHS Trust mental hospital at Leavesden look as if they are part of an industrial complex. About a hundred years old, the hospital was originally called the Metropolitan District Asylum for Imbeciles. The chimneys are a relatively recent addition.

Tower, Shenley Hospital ⑤ J6a to J7 ; 4m E

The services tower of Shenley Mental Hospital. The hospital grounds and buildings are laid out around it like a garden city, built in the neo-Georgian style. The grounds contain Porter's Park, a house which originally belonged to the famous architect Nicholas Hawksmoor, who helped Christopher Wren at St Paul's. It has been so extensively rebuilt over the years that he would not now recognise it.

JUNCTIONS

Watford area

Junction 5
Access to the A41, which runs parallel to the motorway at this point; the exit for Harrow

Junction 6
The A405 Watford to St Albans road crosses the motorway.

Junction 6a
The M1 crosses the M25 London orbital motorway. Access to the M25 for southbound travellers only at this complex junction.

Junction 7
The M10 starts here and finishes three miles away south of St Albans. Southbound access only.

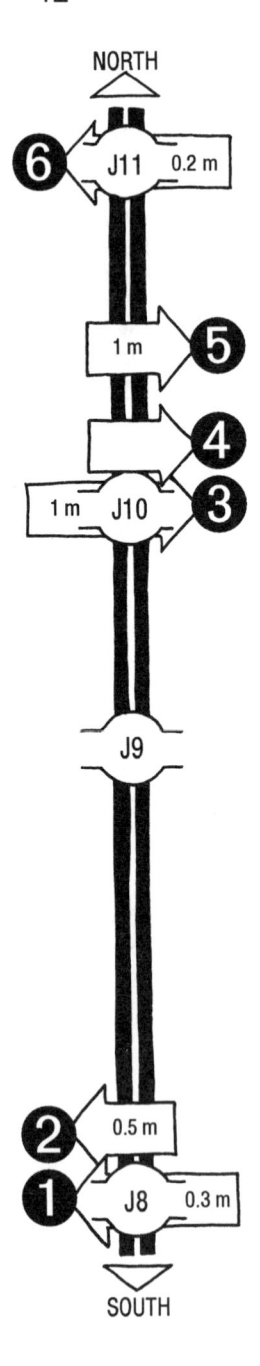

BP House   At J8; 0.3m W

Long and relatively low, this building set in the fields between the motorway and the town of Hemel Hempstead is the head office of BP Oil UK Ltd. It is built of Bath stone, and was opened in 1988. The size is deceptive — 1500 employees are accommodated here.

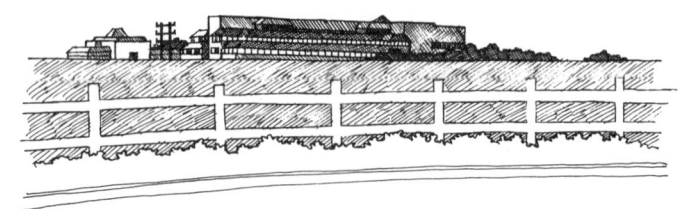

Buncefield oil distribution centre   0.5m N J8; 4m S J9; 0.5m W

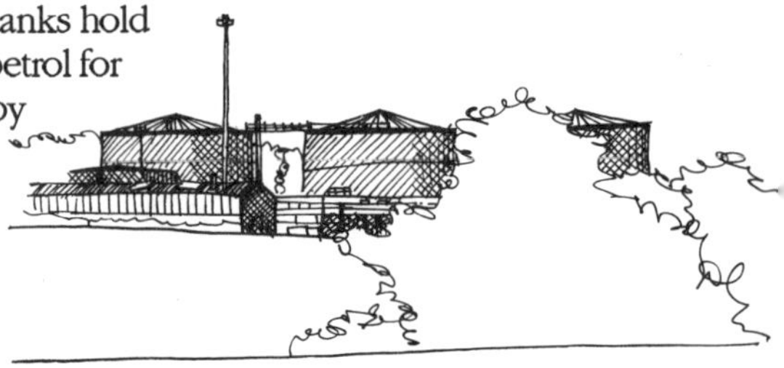

The storage tanks hold fuel oil and petrol for distribution by road tanker to garages and other users in north London and the Home Counties. Oil is brought to the tanks by pipeline. BP, whose head office is nearby (see above), operates the depot.

Luton Hoo   At J10; 1m E

The beautiful house of Luton Hoo remains tantalisingly out of sight from the motorway, but parts of the famous grounds can be seen. These were laid out by Lancelot Brown, who became known as 'Capability' Brown because he would inspect an estate and then declare whether or not he thought it had 'the capability of improvement'. He was considered to be the most outstanding of all eighteenth-century landscape gardeners, and a Brown garden was then the height of fashion.

BEDFORDSHIRE — M1

Luton Hoo houses the Wernher Collection of old-master paintings, tapestries, china, bronzes, and many jewelled ornaments made by Fabergé for the Russian Imperial family.

Stockwood Park ④ 0.5m N J10 ; 3m S J11 ; adjacent E

The golf course is in the grounds of what was claimed to be the finest building in Luton — Stockwood House. We are unable to judge this, because the house was demolished in 1964. Fortunately the stable block and other outbuildings were spared, and now house a thriving craft museum, workshops and an interesting collection of horse-drawn vehicles.

Luton ⑤ 1.5m N J10 ; 2m S J11 ; 1m E

Luton became famous for industry based on the plaiting of straw to make hats. This activity was first noted in the seventeenth century, and by the nineteenth century it had developed to the stage where the town was the national supplier of straw hats, which were then very popular. Hat-making is still carried on, but engineering has taken over as the main industry.

Luton has been the home of Vauxhall Cars, now a part of the American General Motors company, since 1905. The main factory is near the centre of the town, but you can see the massive parts warehouse about 2 miles north of Junction 11.

Luton Airport handles over three million passengers per year, mainly on holiday charter flights.

Luton and Dunstable Hospital ⑥ At J11 ; 0.2m W

The main general hospital for the area, operated by the Luton and Dunstable Hospital NHS Trust.

JUNCTIONS
Luton area

Junction 8
A414 to Hemel Hempstead

Junction 9
The A5 London to Holyhead road crosses the M1 here. It runs close to the M1 into the Midlands, and then follows the route of the Roman Watling Street until Telford.

Junction 10
A1081 to Luton and Luton Airport via a short motorway spur to Junction 10a.

Junction 11
Access to the A505 between Dunstable and Luton

M1 — BEDFORDSHIRE

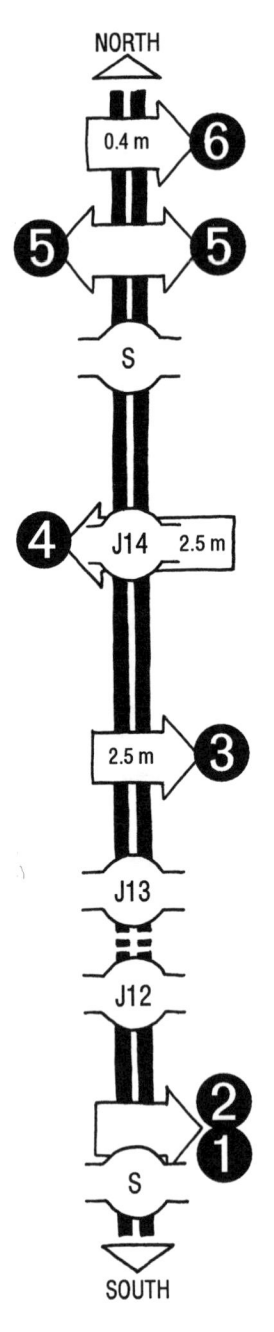

Chiltern Hills ①

The hills you see here are the Chilterns. They are mainly chalk, and form the northern boundary of the Thames valley. Although not particularly high, they offer some pleasant walking, with fine views from such vantage points as the Dunstable Downs and the strangely named Sharpenhoe Clanger, just north of Luton. An ancient road, the Ridgeway, runs along the top.

Railway ② 3m N J11 ; 2m S J12 ; adjacent E

This is the same track which runs beside the M1 at the London end — the London–Luton–Bedford–Leicester–Nottingham line. Here it adjoins the motorway for just a few hundred metres as they share the gap through the Chiltern Hills.

Cranfield ③ 2m N J 13 ; 3m S J 14 ; 2.5m E

The buildings visible from the road are a new science park on the edge of Cranfield airfield. The airfield was opened in 1937 as an RAF bomber station. It became a night-fighter operational training base early in the Second World War.

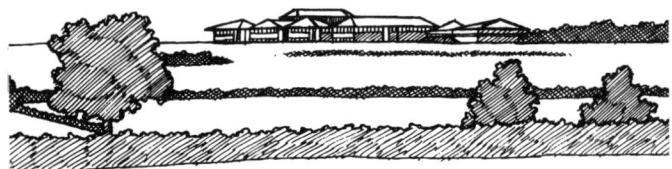

In 1946 the College of Aeronautics was founded here; this has steadily expanded and broadened its interests to become the Cranfield Institute of Technology. The Institute is a postgraduate centre for teaching and research in engineering, technology, management and public policy. A science park has sprung up around the Institute. The airfield remains in use by light aircraft, and serves recreational fliers and business users from the Milton Keynes area.

BUCKINGHAMSHIRE — M1

Milton Keynes ④ At J14; 2m W

Milton Keynes is a complex mixture of a large new town and several existing small towns and villages. It was started in 1967 and has been growing ever since. It is devoid of prominent landmarks, so its very existence is almost undetectable from the M1, even though the motorway passes within a mile or so of the centre.

Population 148,000, and counting.

Great Ouse ⑤ 3.75m N J14; 8.5m S J15; crosses

The Great Ouse river rises a few miles to the west of the M1, at the foot of the Chiltern Hills. It flows in a leisurely manner across East Anglia, passing through Bedford, Huntingdon and Ely before entering the sea at King's Lynn, on the Wash. The lakes which are seen just to the west of the motorway are man-made — mainly old sand and gravel pits — but the Great Ouse also flows through them, and they now play an important part in flood protection for the area. The lakes are a wildfowl sanctuary.

Gayhurst House ⑥ 4.5m N J14; 7.5m S J15; 0.4m E

Gayhurst House is most easily found by looking for the tower of St Peter's Church, Gayhurst. The house can then be seen just to the left of the church, nestling behind trees. It has a long and interesting history:

Apparently the original house was given to Francis Drake by Elizabeth I as a reward for his round-the-world voyage, but Drake didn't want it and sold it the very next day to William Mulso. Mulso can't have been very impressed

JUNCTIONS

Milton Keynes area

Toddington services

Junction 12
A5120 to Ampthill and Dunstable

Junction 13
A421 to Bedford and Milton Keynes

Junction 14
A509 for Milton Keynes and Newport Pagnell

Newport Pagnell services
Britain's first motorway service area. It was a novelty when opened in 1960, a year after the first section of the M1, and families would come here for an evening out.

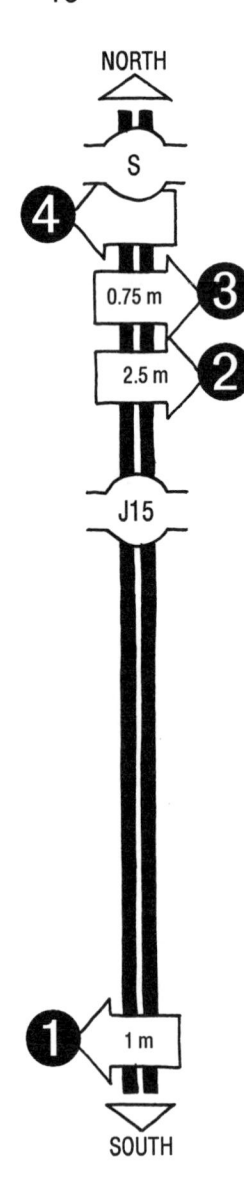

with that house either, because he soon replaced it with the basis of the one which can be seen today.

Building began on the present house in 1597 and was completed by William Mulso's son-in-law, Sir Everard Digby. However, Sir Everard was not to enjoy living here for long; as one of Guy Fawkes' associates in the gunpowder plot of 1605, he was caught, locked in the Tower of London for two months, and then hanged.

The house and estate have been altered over the centuries. In 1763 the grounds were laid out to the design of Lancelot 'Capability' Brown, the famous landscape gardener. The most obvious changes to the house were the flamboyant additions by Lord Carrington in the 1860s. His architect was William Burges, who has been described as 'a draughtsman of grotesque exuberant fantasy'.

St James the Great, Hanslope ❶

6.25m N J14; 5.75m S J15; 1m W

The steeple of St James' is claimed to be the finest in Buckinghamshire. It is over 400 years old, but parts of the church itself are far older, having been started in late Norman times. The steeple was originally 200 ft (60 m) high, but rebuilding and various repairs have left it a little lower now.

Northampton ❷

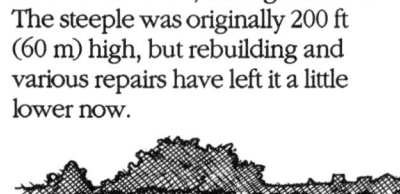

J15 to J16; 2.5m E

Northampton was a very important town in the Middle Ages, and was then surrounded by a fortifying wall. During the Civil War it was a stronghold of support for Cromwell's forces, and when Charles II got the throne back in 1660 he ordered the wall to be demolished. However, Charles acknowledged the economic importance of the town itself, and after being largely destroyed by fire in 1675 it was immediately rebuilt under Act of Parliament, with help from the king.

NORTHAMPTONSHIRE — M1

Northampton became famous and prosperous through the manufacture of leather goods, especially boots and shoes. It is reported that its products shod Cromwell's army, and by Victorian times it was supplying much of the British Empire with footwear. Today there are still many leather firms and shoe shops, but many of the goods are imported.

Population 154,000.

St Benedict, Northampton ③

2m N J15 ; 4m S J16 ; 0.75m E

A modern brick-built church in a good position on the hillside. It has an uncompromisingly industrial air about it, but no doubt will acquire distinction with the passage of time.

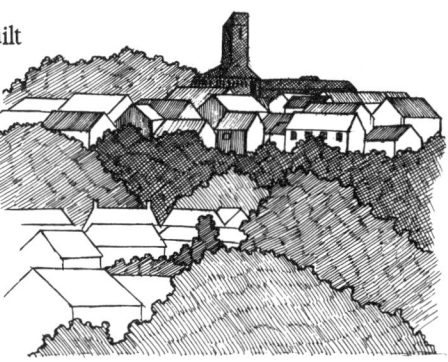

Rothersthorpe locks ④

2.25m N J15 ; 3.75m S J16 ; adjacent W

Just south of Rothersthorpe services you can get a fleeting glimpse of a flight of thirteen locks on the Northampton branch of the Grand Union Canal. This arm of the canal comes from Gayton Junction, not far from the top of the locks, and drops down into Northampton where it connects with the navigable River Nene.

JUNCTIONS

Northampton area

Junction 15
A508: the main turning for Northampton

Rothersthorpe services

M1 — NORTHAMPTONSHIRE

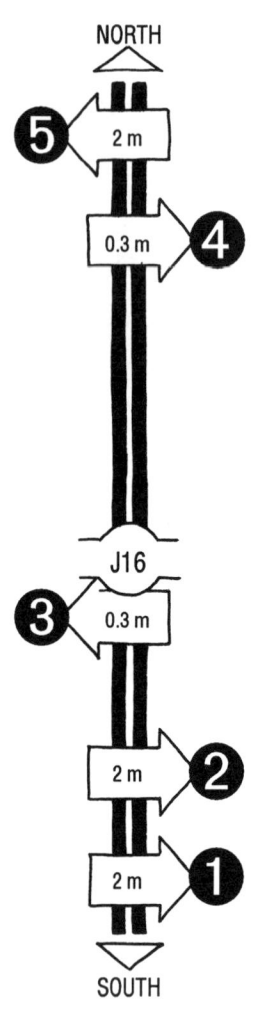

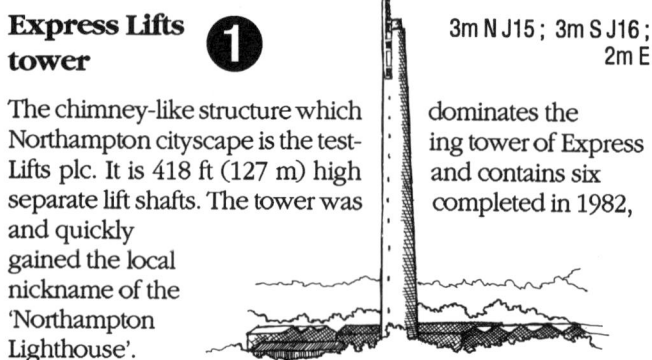

Express Lifts tower ❶

3m N J15; 3m S J16; 2m E

The chimney-like structure which dominates the Northampton cityscape is the testing tower of Express Lifts plc. It is 418 ft (127 m) high and contains six separate lift shafts. The tower was completed in 1982, and quickly gained the local nickname of the 'Northampton Lighthouse'.

Hospitals, Northampton ❷

4m N J15; 2m S J16; 2m E

Just on the northern side of Northampton you will see a collection of large buildings along the ridge of a hill, with a white one standing out particularly clearly. This is the St Crispin's / Princess Marina Hospital complex. St Crispin's was originally built as Berrywood Asylum in 1876, but much has been added to it since then. The Princess Marina Hospital is much newer, dating from 1964–72. Both hospitals were for psychiatric patients, and current policies in the treatment of mental health have led to many of the buildings becoming vacant.

Bugbrooke Mill ❸

5.5m N J15; 0.5m S J16; 0.3m W

Bugbrooke Flour Mill stands beside the River Nene, a prominent landmark set in the flat Northamptonshire farmland. There has been a mill here for over 900 years, as the Domesday Book shows.

NORTHAMPTONSHIRE — M1

The major part of the present mill dates only from 1975. It is run by Heygates, the largest independent millers in England. The Heygate family has a long tradition of farming and milling in the area, starting in 1562.

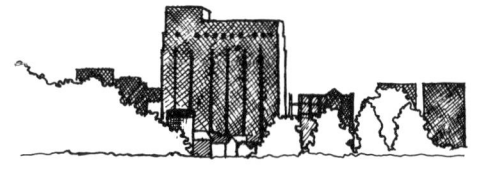

Bugbrooke Mill grinds wheat at the rate of more than ten tonnes per hour, and processes many other cereals for specialised markets. It also houses an extensive food laboratory and a test and development bakery.

> **JUNCTIONS**
>
> **Northampton/ Daventry area**
>
> **Junction 16**
> Here the M1 crosses the A45, which runs almost directly east–west from Felixstowe to Birmingham.

Brockhall Hall ④   3.5m N J16 ; 5.5m S J17 ; 0.3m E

Brockhall Hall can be glimpsed through the trees. It dates from Elizabethan times, but has been altered and added to over the years.

Daventry Radio Station ⑤   4.5m N J16 ; 4.5m S J17 ; 2m W

The mass of masts on the top of Borough Hill (650 ft; 200 m) marks what was until recently the BBC's World Service short-wave broadcasting station. At the time of writing, the future of the masts is uncertain.

The Daventry station was the BBC's first high-power transmitter and was by far the biggest radio station in the world when it was opened in 1925. Radio enthusiasts and historians are applying pressure for the installations to be preserved.

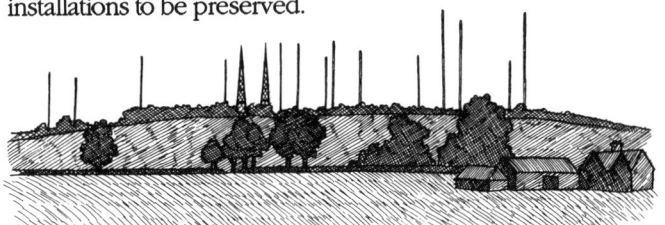

Borough Hill is also the site of an Iron Age hill fort, and provided a camp site for the Royalist army before the battle of Naseby in 1645.

M1 — NORTHAMPTONSHIRE

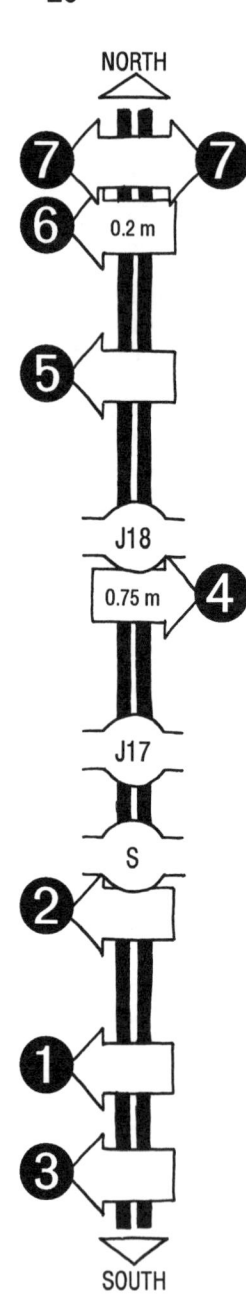

Railway ①
4m N J16 to 2m S J17 ; adjacent W

This is the main line linking London with Birmingham and the North-west.

Roman road ②

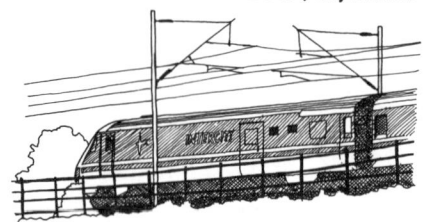

For most of the way between Junctions 16 and 18 the M1 runs beside Watling Street, the Roman road which ran from the Kent coast to Holyhead in North Wales. Watling Street north of London has become the A5, and for most of its length it displays the characteristic straightness for which the Roman road-builders are famous.

Grand Union Canal ③
4m N J16 ; 4m S J17 ; adj. W

The main line of the Grand Union Canal runs close to the motorway here, and the Leicester branch crosses further up at Watford Gap. The Grand Union is actually a group of canals which serve the whole of the Midlands as well as linking the Thames with the Trent and the Severn. They were built at the end of the eighteenth century, in the later part of the great canal boom.

St Margaret, Crick ④
1.5 m N J17 ; 0.5m S J18 ; 0.75m E

This is an appealing small church from the Decorated period (about 1290–1350). Much of the original fabric has survived without restoration.

NORTHAMPTONSHIRE — M1

Rugby Radio Station ⑤ J18 to 1m S J19 ; adjacent W

This mass of masts is the commercial and maritime radio station now run by British Telecom. The site covers 1650 acres spanning the Northamptonshire/Warwickshire border, and from the road it is quite difficult to judge the scale of the installations. There are 200 masts in all, the twelve largest of which are each 820 ft (250 m) high and weigh 200 tonnes. At one time these were the tallest structures in Britain. Even the 'small' masts are 150 ft (45 m) high. The masts support about 3.5 miles of copper wire.

JUNCTIONS

Rugby area

Watford Gap services

Junction 17
Northbound access only to the short M45 motorway towards Coventry

Junction 18
A5 for Hinckley and A428 for Rugby

Lilbourne All Saints, motte and bailey ⑥ 3m N J18 ; 0.5m S J19 ; 0.2m W

Lilbourne Church sits in a meadow beside the M1, in a site of great antiquity. The church dates from the thirteenth century, but the mounds to the right of of it are much older than that. They were probably originally Roman burial mounds, but shortly after 1066 the Normans built a motte-and-bailey castle on them. In their simplest form these castles consisted of a mound with a strong wooden tower on the top. Here at Lilbourne there seems to have been a tower on each mound, with walls linking them to form a small but secure castle.

River Avon ⑦ 3.25m N J18 ; 0.25m S J19 ; crosses

The River Avon rises close by to the east and flows into the Severn at Tewkesbury in Gloucestershire.

M1 — LEICESTERSHIRE

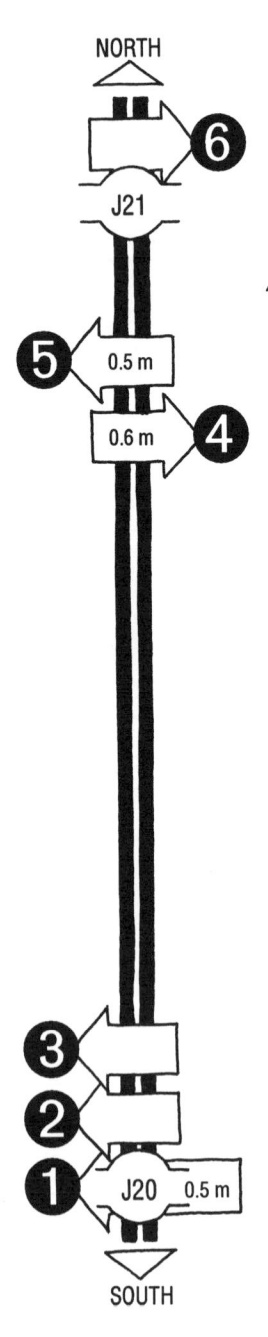

St Mary, Lutterworth ❶   At J20 ; 0.5m W

A large late-13th and 14th-century parish church. The tower is later, because the original spire collapsed in 1703. John Wycliffe, the controversial but popular religious reformer who attacked many of his fellow clergy for putting wealth above religion, was the rector of St Mary's from 1374 to 1384. During his time here he supervised the first translation of the Bible into English, and there is a memorial to him in the church.

BOCM Silcock Ltd plant ❷   0.5m N J20 ; 10.25m S J21 ; adjacent W

A large plant operated by British Oil and Cake Mills Ltd, the country's leading manufacturer of animal feedstuffs. Here cereals and oil seeds are turned into food for all types of cattle, sheep and poultry.

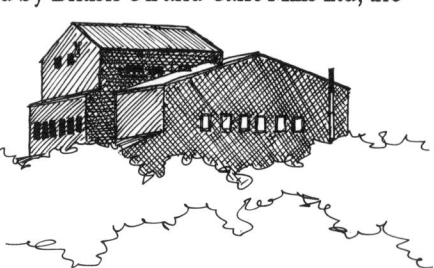

Chimney with aerials, Lutterworth ❸   1m N J20 ; 9.75m S J21 ; adjacent W

This chimney is part of the wartime Alfred Herbert machine tool factory, which now belongs to the Devlieg Machine Co Ltd. Herberts, based in Coventry, established this factory at Lutterworth in 1941 to avoid the wartime blitz.

The top of the chimney is rented by Cellnet and carries a number of their aerials.

LEICESTERSHIRE — M1   23

St Peter, Whetstone ④   8.75m N J 20 ; 2m S J21 ; 0.6m E

An early fourteenth-century parish church, but much renewed. The steeple was completely reconstructed in 1856.

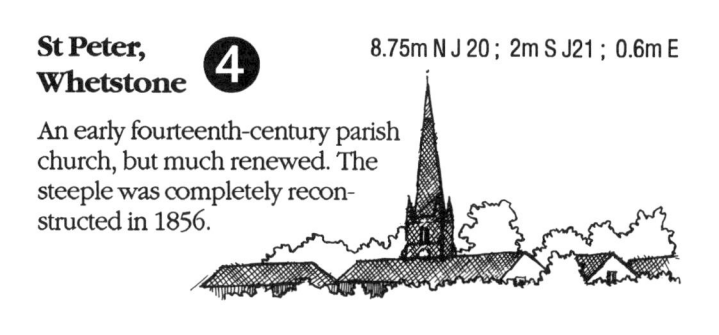

Narborough Hospital ⑤   9.25m N J20 ; 1.5m S J21 ; 0.5m W

The twin towers are part of a large hospital complex comprising the Leicester Health Authority's mental health unit. Most of it was constructed at the beginning of this century.

Mattel Toys warehouse ⑥   0.25m N J21 ; 7.75m S J22 ; adjacent E

It may come as a surprise to some that the real home of Barbie and the Masters of the Universe is this huge warehouse and distribution centre for Mattel Toys. This is big business: the floor-to-ceiling racking can store 10,000 pallets.

JUNCTIONS

Lutterworth/ Leicester area

Junction 19
M6 to Birmingham and the Northwest; northbound access only. This junction is now being altered to provide access to the A14, the new M1–A1 link road.

Junction 20
A427 for Lutterworth and Market Harborough

Junction 21
A46 for Leicester and M69 for Coventry

M1 — LEICESTERSHIRE

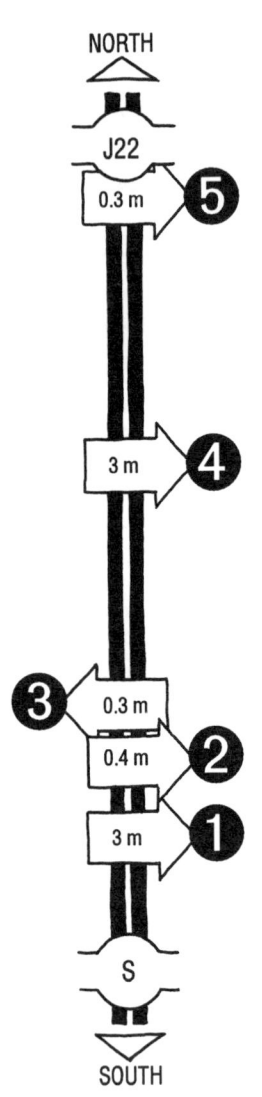

Leicester ① J21 to 3m N J21; 3m E

Leicester was an important town in Roman times, and there are still some large chunks of Roman buildings to be seen. A thousand or so years later, the Norman invaders used it as a power base, the first Earl of Leicester building the Great Hall as his administrative centre in the twelfth century. It is still used as a courthouse today. During the industrial revolution Leicester grew greatly through the introduction of mechanised knitting, and the town is still a centre for knitwear, hosiery and footwear.

Population 280,000

British Shoe Corporation Distribution Centre ② 2.25m N J21; 5.75m S J22; 0.4m E

The view of the British Shoe Corporation's warehouse which you get from the motorway does not do justice to the scale of the place itself. From here a million pairs of shoes are distributed each week to over 2,000 shops. Most of the familiar names of shoe shops in the British high streets are supplied: Curtess, Dolcis, Freeman Hardy and Willis, Manfield, Saxone, Shoe City and Trueform.

Kirby Muxloe Castle ③ 2.75m N J21; 5.25m S J22; 0.3m W

Lord Hastings, a powerful local nobleman, started to build this castle in 1480, but it was abandoned long before it was

LEICESTERSHIRE — M1

completed. The reason for this shows just how precarious life could be at the end of the Middle Ages, even for someone who had attained vast wealth and status. Hastings was one of the principal supporters of the King, Edward IV. Unfortunately, Edward died in 1483, and Richard, Duke of York, had his eyes on the throne; Richard had Hastings executed without trial, presumably to reduce opposition when he seized the throne to become Richard III.

Kirby Muxloe Castle is quite unusual in that it is constructed mainly of brick, rather than stone.

Old John Tower ④   5m N J21 ; 3m S J22 ; 3m E

The Old John Tower stands on a hilltop about three miles to the east of the road. It was built in 1786 by the 5th Earl of Stamford as a memorial to an aged family retainer, the eponymous Old John, who had the misfortune to be killed by a flagpole falling from a bonfire during a party to celebrate the Earl's eldest son's twenty-first birthday. It should act as a grim reminder about the foolishness of constructing bonfires around flagpoles ...

The Old John Tower marks the highest point of Bradgate Country Park. Bradgate was the birthplace of the tragic Lady Jane Grey, who was very briefly Queen of England in 1553.

Quarry Hill, Markfield ⑤   7.5m N J21 ; 0.5m S J22 ; 0.3m E

The steep hill and rock outcrops conceal a large quarry at the top. It is now disused, but has left the hill almost like a dead volcano, with a deep water-filled crater at the top.

JUNCTIONS

Leicester area

Leicester Forest East services

Junction 22
Here the motorway crosses the A50 Leicester to Stoke-on-Trent road.

M1 — LEICESTERSHIRE

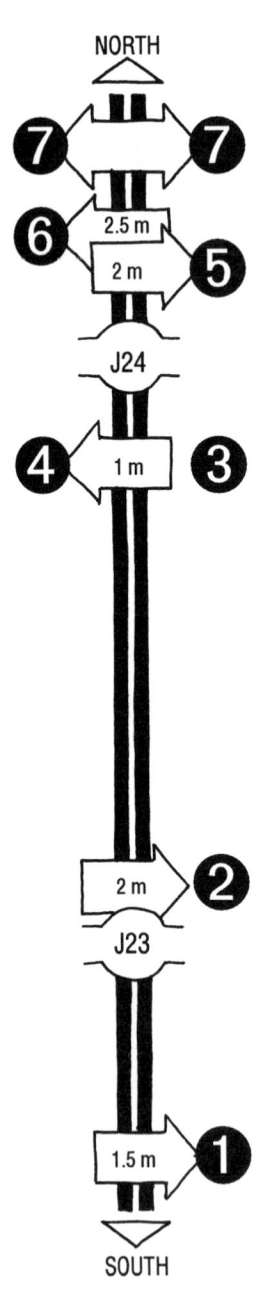

Beacon Hill ❶   2.5m N J22 ; 2m S J23 ; 1.5m E

The highest point in the area (850 ft; 250 m). There is nowhere higher to the east until you reach the Ural Mountains in Russia.

Loughborough ❷   Around J23 ; 2m E

Loughborough is the third largest town in Leicestershire (after Leicester and Hinckley). It prospered mainly through the woollen textile industry, but now is more famous for the Loughborough University of Technology, the buildings of which can be seen from the motorway.

Site of Kegworth air crash ❸   5m N J23 ; 1m S J24

On 8 January 1989, a British Midland Airways Boeing 737-400, G-OBME, developed problems with one of its two engines while flying from Heathrow to Belfast. The aircraft diverted to East Midlands Airport, which is almost next to the M1 at Kegworth. Tragically, during the emergency the remaining sound engine was shut down, and the aircraft landed short, crashing onto the motorway. Forty-seven of the 125 passengers and crew on board were killed. There is no marker, so the exact site is difficult to locate. However, there is a small commemorative plaque on the bridge nearby.

East Midlands International Airport ❹   5m N J23 ; 1m S J24 ; 1m W

East Midlands is England's third largest regional airport. Sightseers are encouraged: there is the Aeropark open-air museum, as well as a visitor centre with exhibits and an airport viewing area.

The airport opened in 1965, but flying had gone on here long before that: it is built on the site of Castle Donington RAF aerodrome, which dates from the Second World War. In its RAF days it was an operational training unit for bombers (mainly Wellingtons), and later a transport unit.

DERBYSHIRE — M1

All Saints', Sawley (see page 28)

River Trent

Ratcliffe-on-Soar Power Station

Ratcliffe-on-Soar Power Station ⑤

1m N J24 ; 4m S J25 ; 2m E

Opened in 1970, Ratcliffe-on-Soar is a vast power station which can produce enough electricity to meet the needs of two million people. It burns coal at the rate of 13.5 tonnes a minute, with a consistently high level of efficiency. In the 1970s and 80s the coal was mined locally. By its sheer size, a power station such as this must inevitably dominate the view. However, attempts to lessen this effect have been made by landscaping and planting thousands of trees. It's the thought that counts.

Castle Donington Power Station ⑥

1m N J24 ; 4m S J25 ; 2.5m W

By power-station standards Castle Donington is now relatively small, but when it opened in 1951 it was the biggest in Europe. Like its larger brother across the motorway at Ratcliffe, this station was designed to burn local coal.

River Trent ⑦

2m N J24 ; 3m S J25 ; crosses

The River Trent, 168 miles long, is the third longest river in England. It rises north of Stoke and flows into the Humber. Here it forms the border between Leicestershire and Derbyshire. It has always been an important trade route, even as long ago as the Bronze Age. To the east of the motorway at Sawley it is navigable as the Trent Navigation for almost 100 miles — as far as the Humber. Half a mile to the west of the M1, the River Trent becomes unnavigable, but boats can continue their journey on the Trent and Mersey Canal.

From the motorway you can see the locks in the Sawley Cut of the Trent Navigation, which by-passes an unnavigable section of the river, seen flowing over the weir to the left of the cut.

JUNCTIONS

Loughborough area

Junction 23
A512 Loughborough to Ashby

Junction 23a
New junction for A42/M42 to Birmingham

Junction 24
A453 for East Midlands airport, and A6, the main route from London to the North-west before the M6 opened.

M1 — DERBYSHIRE

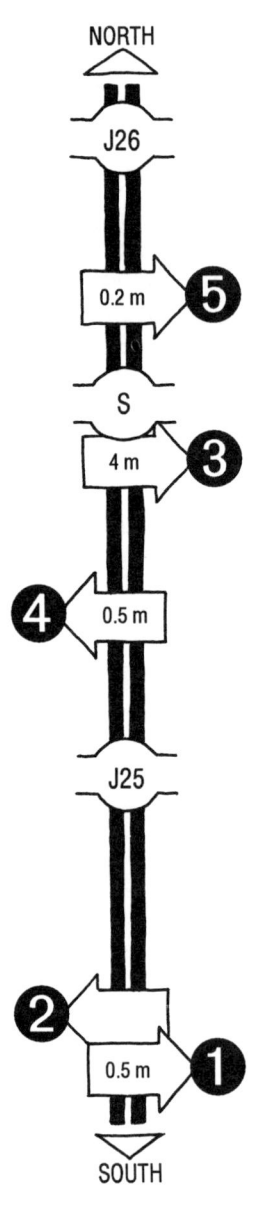

All Saints, Sawley ①
2.25m N J24 ; 2.75m S J25 ; 0.5m E

The church at Sawley, All Saints, provides a great contrast with the giant bulk of Ratcliffe power station behind it. The earliest parts are Norman. *(Illustration on page 27.)*

Church Wilne reservoir ②
2.75m N J24 ; 2.25m S J25 ; adjacent W

The Church Wilne pump-storage reservoir is alongside the motorway — it is a huge concrete bowl which was constructed quite recently for Severn-Trent Water. The buildings close to the motorway are the treatment plant for chlorination, fluoridation, etc., but your eye will probably be most attracted by the mushroom of water pumping up into the reservoir itself. The plant supplies the water needs of Long Eaton and nearby areas.

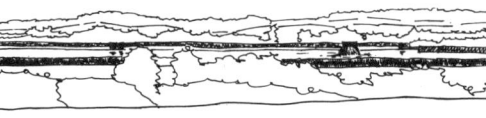

Above: reservoir; below: treatment works

Nottingham ③
J25 to J26 ; 4m E

Nottingham was an important mediaeval trading centre. Later, lace became its speciality, and is still made in the city.

However, Nottingham's most famous product is the legend of Robin Hood. Whoever he was, the man in the green suit seems to have left few hard facts about his life and times, so the legend-makers, aided and abetted by the film industry, have filled in the gaps with enthusiasm. Certainly, there is no doubt that the motorway passes over ground which was once covered by Sherwood Forest, so maybe Robin really did come out of the woods to confound the Sheriff of Nottingham from time to time.

Population 280,000.

NOTTINGHAMSHIRE — M1

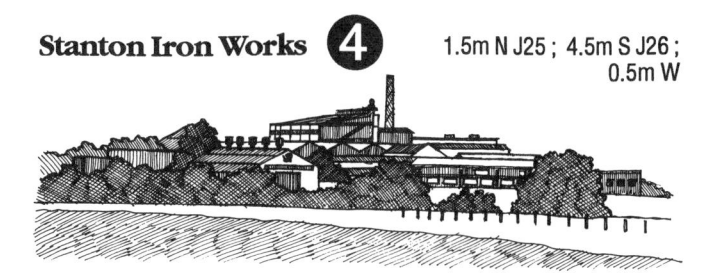

Stanton Iron Works ④   1.5m N J25 ; 4.5m S J26 ; 0.5m W

Ironworks have stood on this site for 150 years, but there have been many changes to them. When we first devised this book there were works right alongside the M1, but these were demolished in 1991. Stanton plc's main business is the production of iron and concrete pipes for the water and construction industry, and iron lining segments for tunnels.

For a long time a subsidiary of Stewarts and Lloyds, Stanton was nationalised in 1967, becoming part of the British Steel Corporation. It was privatised in 1985, and effectively taken over by the French *Pont-à-Mousson* company.

JUNCTIONS
Nottingham area
Junction 25 A52 for Nottingham and Derby
Trowell services
Junction 26 A610 to Nottingham

All Saints, Strelley and Strelley Hall ⑤   4.5m N J25 ; 1.5m S J26 ; 0.2m E

Strelley village is still almost unspoilt. Endowed by Samson de Strelley in 1356, All Saints is historically important: the chancel furnishings provide the most complete example in Nottinghamshire of gifts bestowed by local gentry on their parish church. Many members of the Strelley family are buried here, including Sir Robert Strelley, who fought at Agincourt in 1415.

The current Strelley Hall, a large plain brick house of two and a half storeys in a landscaped park, was built 1789–92 by Thomas Gardner for Thomas Webb Edge. Gardner built many such plain but stylish Georgian houses. The stables include parts of the earlier mediaeval house. The Hall is now occupied by a computer company, PAFEC Computer Solutions.

M1 — NOTTINGHAMSHIRE

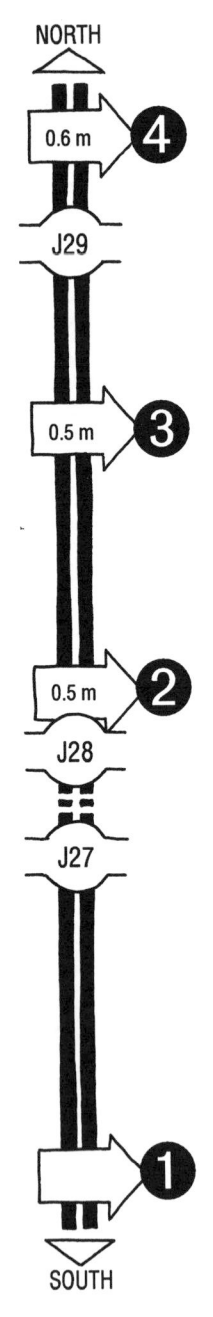

Watnall brickworks ❶

2.5m N J26 ; 5.5m S J27 ;
adj. E

Four tall chimneys mark the old Watnall brickworks. The works are now disused, and the condition of the chimneys is deteriorating steadily, so this landmark will probably disappear before too long.

The Great Yellow Pipe Factory ❷

0.5m N J28 ; 6.5m S J29 ;
0.5m E

Du Pont (UK) Limited. Here is Du Pont's Hilcote plant which produces polythene pipe under the trade-name Aldyl for the gas industry. This has virtually replaced metal for gas supply, and now thousands of miles of pipes from here lie under the pavements of the nation.

Hardwick Hall and Hardwick Old Hall ❸

5m N J28 ; 2m S J29 ;
0.5m E

Hardwick Hall is a magnificent Elizabethan country house, designed by Robert Smythson, and distinguished by its six towers. It is unusual in that it has not been re-modelled or 'improved' since it was built in the sixteenth century. It was

Hardwick Hall

DERBYSHIRE — M1

Hardwick Old Hall

commissioned by Bess of Hardwick, a local woman who achieved great wealth and status by surviving four husbands, and she lived here in grand style. She had been born in the nearby manor house which she subsequently extended to become the Old Hall. This is now in ruins, which you can still see just to the north of the Hall. Bess' taste for construction was considerable — she also built the original house at Chatsworth.

The Hall and surrounding 300-acre gardens are in the care of English Heritage. They are well worth visiting. Although the gardens are open throughout the year, the hall is not open every day, so check before making a journey there.

JUNCTIONS

Mansfield area

Junction 27
A608 for Heanor and Hucknall

Junction 28
A38 Bodmin (in Cornwall) to Mansfield

Junction 29
A617 to Chesterfield and Mansfield

Sutton Scarsdale Hall ④

1.25m N J29 ; 5.25m S J30 ; 0.6m E

A handsome building with an impressive classical facade overlooking the motorway. It is just far enough away for you not to realise that it is a ruin. Sutton Scarsdale Hall was built for Lord Scarsdale in 1724, but fell into disrepair shortly after the 1914–1918 war. What is left is now in the care of English Heritage, who must be wondering just what can be done with it.

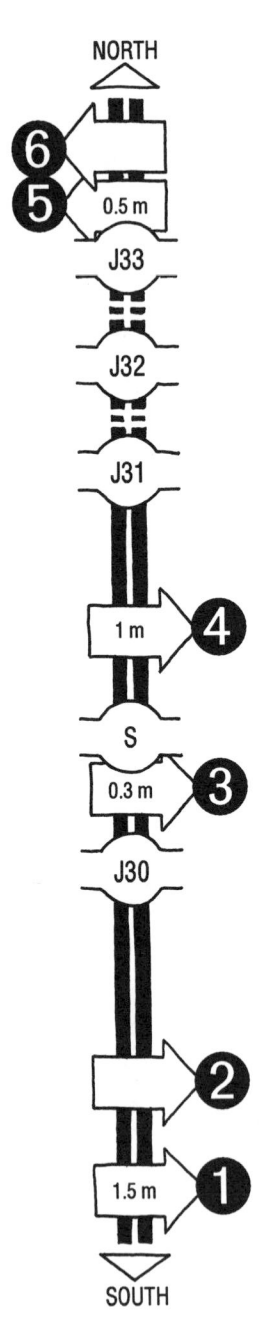

M1 — DERBYSHIRE

Bolsover Castle ❶   1.75m N J29 ; 4.5m S J30 ; 1.5m E

A vast mansion built by the Cavendish family on the site of a former mediaeval castle. Constructed between 1608 and 1640, the castle is managed by English Heritage, and is open to the public from 10 am to 6 pm in summer and 10 am to 4 pm in winter, when it is also shut on Mondays. Bolsover Castle now commands an unrivalled view of the nearby Coalite plant, which is at the centre of controversy about alleged emissions of the poisonous chemical dioxin.

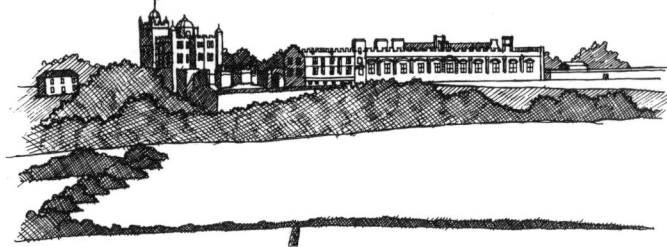

Markham mine ❷   3m N J29 ; 3.25m S J30 ; adjacent E

British Coal. Central area coal measures, East Pennine coalfield. As this book goes to press, Markham appears likely to close.

Barlborough Hall ❸   1.25m N J30 ; 4.25m S J31 ; 0.3m E

An Elizabethan house built by Sir Francis Rodes in 1583–84. Rodes was a judge whose lucrative law practice enabled him to build Barlborough and to own other estates in the area. His appointment was as 'Justice of the Common Pleas', and he was one of the judges at the trial of Mary Queen of Scots in 1586.

SOUTH YORKSHIRE — M1

The compact square design of Barlborough Hall is quite unusual, but it shares some features with Hardwick Hall, a few miles further south.

Barlborough Hall is now a Roman Catholic prep school.

Kiveton Park mine ④   3.25m N J30 ; 2m S J31 ; 1m E

British Coal. South Yorkshire area coal measures, East Pennine coalfield. As this book goes to press, Kiveton Park appears likely to close.

Conical Furnace, Catcliffe ⑤   0.5m N J33 ; 3m S J34 ; 0.5m W

This marks the old Catcliffe glassworks, which date from 1746. It is reputedly the oldest building of its type in Europe. The glassblowers worked at a number of separate hearths around the base of the brick-built cone. Production finally ceased in 1900.

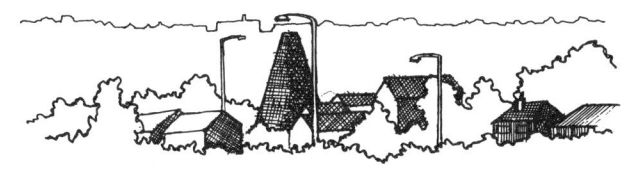

Steel works, Sheffield ⑥   1m N J33 to J34 ; adj. W

Avesta is a new name in Sheffield steel: the result of the 1992 merger between British Stainless plc and a group of Swedish companies. The name comes from the Swedish town of Avesta, Sheffield's Scandinavian counterpart as a major centre of stainless production.

JUNCTIONS

Chesterfield/ Sheffield area

Junction 30
A619 to Chesterfield and Worksop

Woodall service area

Junction 31
A57 to Sheffield and Worksop

Junction 32
M18 to the Northeast

Junction 33
A630; the main route to Sheffield centre from the south.

M1 — SOUTH YORKSHIRE

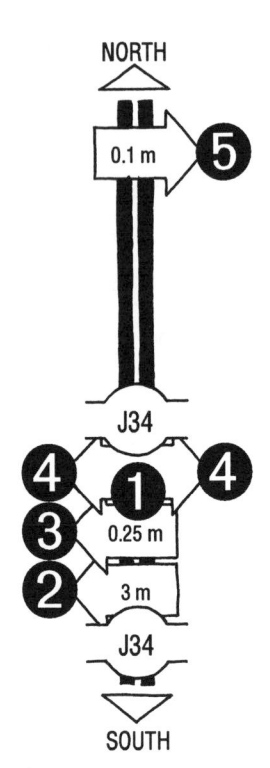

Tinsley Viaduct ❶ At J34

The viaduct is a two-level steel box-girder structure which is three-quarters of a mile long; the M1 uses the top deck, and the lower deck is the non-motorway link between the two roundabouts of Junction 34. It was opened in June 1968, but had to be partially closed in 1973 because of fears about the safety of box-girder bridges. The necessary strengthening work took 6 years to complete. Peregrine falcons overwinter in the two disused cooling towers next to the viaduct. Good views of Sheffield to the west and Rotherham to the east.

Sheffield ❷ At J34; 3m W

A great industrial centre, Sheffield grew because it was close to supplies of coal and iron and is well served by waterways for transportation. It became famous worldwide for its high-quality steel and cutlery. Sheffield hosted the World Student Games in 1991, and the yellow roof supports of the Don Valley Stadium are prominent in the cityscape. The distant hills behind the city mark the edge of the Derbyshire Peak District.

Population 475,000.

Meadowhall shopping and leisure development, Tinsley ❸ At J34; 0.25m W

Meadowhall is a vast shopping mall on the American pattern. Its site was once an area of grim-looking steelworks beside the River Don. There are over 230 shops and stores within the complex, as well as an enormous restaurant area.

SOUTH YORKSHIRE — M1

Meadowhall opened on 4 September 1990, and received over 20 million visitors within its first year.

River Don ④ At J34 ; crosses

The Don flows off the hills of the Peak District and into the River Ouse to the east; it forms part of the River Don Navigation, connecting Sheffield with the Humber.

Thundercliffe Grange ⑤ 2.5m N J34 ; 1.5m S J35 ; 0.1m E

In spite of having had a third floor added, this impressive 200-year-old mansion still shows pleasant proportions. In summer you have to be quick to get a good view of it between the trees. Thundercliffe Grange is now divided into private flats.

JUNCTIONS

Sheffield/ Rotherham area

Junction 34
For Meadowhall, Sheffield and Rotherham. A complex junction straddling the river Don, partly formed by the Tinsley Viaduct.

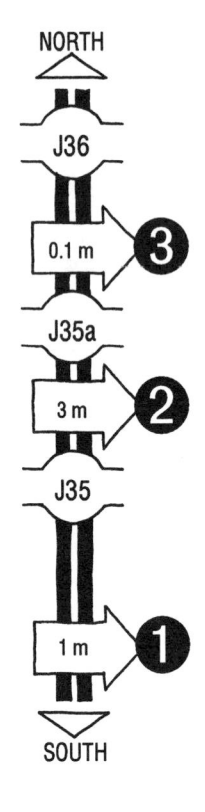

Keppel's Column

2.5m N J34 ; 1.5m S J35 ; 1m E

Admiral Viscount Keppel was an eminent eighteenth-century seaman who got seriously out of royal favour for not trying hard enough when attempting to smite the French in a battle during 1778. He was acquitted at a subsequent court-martial, whereupon his friend, Charles Wentworth, 2nd Marquis of Rockingham, who lived in great style at nearby Wentworth Woodhouse, commemorated the event by modifying a folly that was already being built at this spot and dedicating it to Keppel.

The Column's proportions are rather strange, as it was originally designed to be considerably taller than the 115 ft (35 m) it eventually attained when building finished in 1780. The views from the platform must be stunning, but unfortunately there is now no public access to the top of this prominent landmark.

The architect of the Column was John Carr, one of whose claims to fame is Harewood House. You can see his elegant church at Horbury, a few miles to the north.

Hoober Stand

J35–J35a ; 3m E

Seen from the distance of the M1, this looks rather like a disused windmill. However, it is another of the bizarre monuments erected by the Marquis of Rockingham, who would get

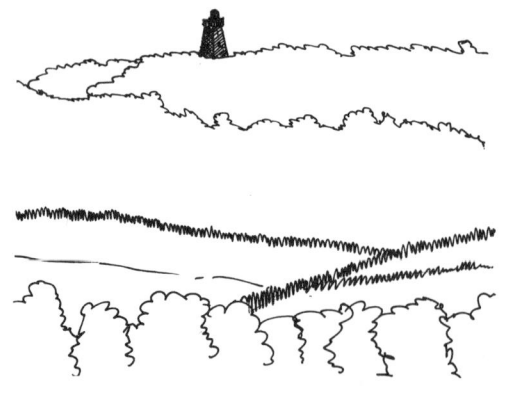

SOUTH YORKSHIRE — M1

his craftsmen hewing stone at only the slightest provocation. His excuse for constructing this extraordinary three-sided tower with its large cupola on top was to celebrate the putting down of the Jacobite rebellion of 1745–6. He had served the Duke of Cumberland during this campaign, and his reward was to be made Marquis. Part of the inscription shows that he had got sucking up to royalty off to a fine art: '*This pyramidall Building was erected by His Majesty's most Dutyfull Subject, Thomas, Marquess of Rockingham, in Grateful Respect to the Preserver of our Religion, Laws and Libertys, King George the Second ...*'.

The Hoober Stand gets its curious name from the simple fact that it stands at the hamlet of Hoober.

Ruins of Tankersley Hall ③

0.75m N J 35a ; 1m S J36 ; 0.1m E

The original Tankersley Hall is more than four hundred years old, but has been in ruins for about three hundred of them. A farmhouse has been built onto part of the old Hall and incorporates some of its stone. The M1 runs through the middle of what were once the Hall grounds, which extended well past the golf course on the other side of the motorway.

JUNCTIONS

Chapeltown area

Junction 35
A629: main exit travelling south for Rotherham.

Junction 35a
A616 for Huddersfield and Manchester

Junction 36
The M1 crosses the A61, the Barnsley to Sheffield road.

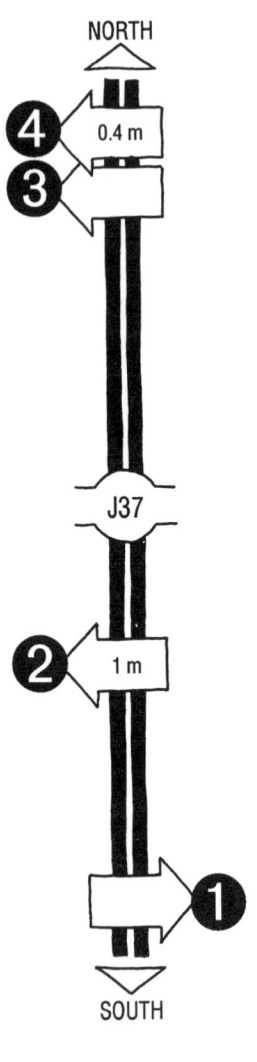

Obelisk, Birdwell ❶

0.25m N J36 ;
3.75m S J37 ;
adjacent E

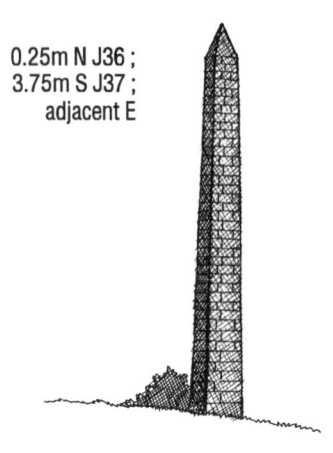

This well-proportioned obelisk rises out of a transport yard close to Junction 36. It is a waymarker inscribed 'Wentworth Castle 3 miles, 1780'. Quite prominent when travelling north, it is easily missed from the southbound carriageway.

Wentworth Castle ❷

2.5m N J36 ; 1.5m S J37 ; 1m W

Started around 1670 as merely a grand house, the building was purchased by Thomas Wentworth in 1708. Wentworth had recently returned from the post of British Ambassador to Berlin, where he had acquired a taste for architectural splendour on a grand scale. He indulged this interest unrestrained, and soon his magnificent house had three new wings, with rooms up to 180 ft (55 m) long. He didn't hold back in the gardens either, constructing a gothic-style castle, two obelisks, a rotunda and a church-like gate lodge.

Wentworth Castle is the stately home you *can* see from the motorway; Wentworth Woodhouse is the one you can't. They were built by different branches of the Woodhouse family, and it isn't hard to imagine that there was a fair element of intra-family competition in their building enterprises.

SOUTH YORKSHIRE — M1

BP Plastics factory ③

3.25m N J37 ; 1.25m S J38 ; adjacent W

The former British Xylonite factory at Kexborough, the birthplace of millions of bin liners, nappy bags, supermarket carriers, food-wrapping film and other twentieth-century delights.

> **JUNCTIONS**
>
> **Barnsley area**
>
> **Junction 37**
> The M1 crosses the A628, which connects Barnsley with Manchester via some wild moorland country.

The factory was joined in 1992 by a huge modern shed in which the Spring Ram company constructs doors.

Birthwaite Hall ④

3.5m N J37 ; 1m S J38 ; 0.4m W

A delightful early eighteenth-century house which was originally owned by John Silvester, who had served his country as Smith to the Tower of London. This was an important post at the time: Silvester was at the head of armaments development in his era, and enjoyed considerable fame as the man who prevented the Dutch fleet from sailing up the Thames by putting a chain across it. Either he was heavily rewarded for this, or his job paid very well, as his house is quite grand by any standards.

M1 — WEST YORKSHIRE

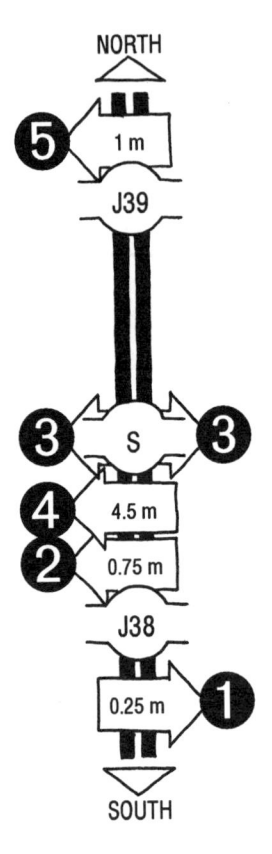

Woolley colliery ❶

3.75m N J37 ; 0.75m S J38 ; 0.25m E

Although this large colliery has been out of production since 1987, the extensive washing plant has continued to process coal from other local pits.

Bretton Hall ❷

0.5m N J38 ; 3m S J39 ; 0.75m W

In winter you can see Bretton Hall, some distance away behind the trees. In summer the Hall is hidden, but you can see the entrance lodge to Bretton Hall Country Park. Bretton Hall was built by Sir Jeffry Wyatville for Sir William Wentworth, cousin of Thomas who built Wentworth Castle. Wyatville was one of the country's leading architects at the time, and among his other works was the rehabilitation of Windsor Castle for George IV.

Bretton Hall College of the University of Leeds now uses the mansion and the modern buildings on the site.

The Yorkshire Sculpture Park occupies part of the Bretton Hall Country Park (the grounds of Bretton Hall); it is free, and well worth a visit.

WEST YORKSHIRE — M1

Railway breathers, Woolley ③

At Woolley Edge services

There is one of these on each side of the carriageway: they provide ventilation for the mile-long railway tunnel on the Leeds–Sheffield line which runs below the Woolley Edge service area.

TV mast, Emley Moor ④

1m N J38 ; 3m S J39 ; 4.5m W

At 1084 ft (330 m), this is the tallest concrete structure in Britain. It replaces a steel mast which collapsed under the weight of ice in 1969. It is operated by the Independent Broadcasting Authority, and transmits both ITV and BBC TV programmes over much of Yorkshire, Nottinghamshire and Lincolnshire.

Viaduct, Calder Grove ⑤

0.5m N J39 ; 2m S J40 ; 1m W

This viaduct, now disused, once carried the railway line which ran into Dewsbury. It is built of the local 'blue' brick, and is really more handsome than first sight suggests.

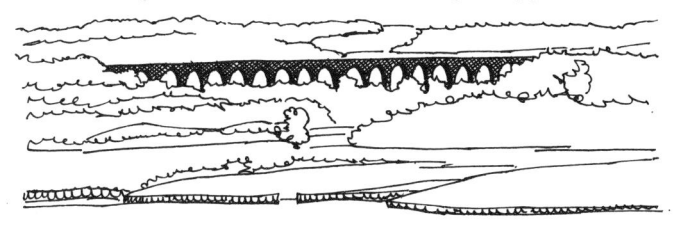

JUNCTIONS

Woolley Edge area

Junction 38
The A637 from Barnsley to Huddersfield crosses the M1 here. This is the northbound exit for the Yorkshire Sculpture Park.

Woolley Edge services

Junction 39
The M1 crosses the A636 Wakefield to Denby Dale road. Exit here for the Yorkshire Sculpture Park when travelling south.

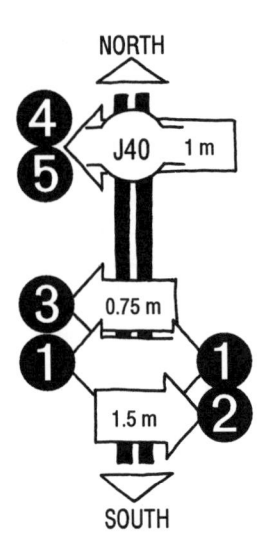

River Calder ①

0.5m N J39 ; 2m S J40 ; crosses

Just north of Junction 39, the M1 crosses the River Calder. At this point it is part of the Calder and Hebble Navigation, which carried industrial goods through Yorkshire until the early 1980s. Now the only vessels that you will see on it are pleasure craft.

Sandal Castle ②

0.5m N J39 ; 2m S J40 ; 1.5m E

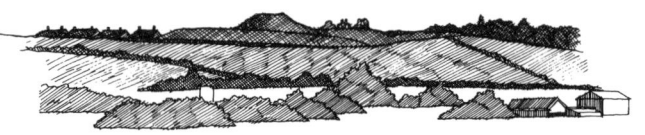

If you look across to the east, you will be able to see the ruins of Sandal Castle on the horizon. These don't look particularly thrilling, but their rather unimpressive appearance hides a long and lurid history. The conquering Normans built a wooden motte-and-bailey castle on this site around the year 1100, but the stone remains which you see date from 1328. Many bloody battles have taken place around the castle, and you are now virtually driving through the field of the battle of Wakefield, which cost 5000 lives during the Wars of the Roses. The useful days of the castle came to an end during the Civil War, when a group of remaining Royalists was defeated here by Cromwell's troops.

You may be able to see the sails of boats in front of the castle remains. These are on the lake in Pugney's Country Park. It covers 80 acres, and is open to the public for a wide variety of water sports, including windsurfing, dinghy sailing and canoeing. Equipment for all this can be hired at the park.

St Peter and St Leonard, Horbury ③

1m N J39 ; 1.5m S J40 ; 0.75m W

Built by the Horbury architect John Carr between 1790 and 1791, in the classical style. You will easily spot its four-tiered tower above the trees. Carr was twice Lord Mayor of York, but remained very fond of his home town: this church was his gift to the residents of Horbury, and he met the cost of £8000 entirely from his own pocket. Baring-Gould wrote the

WEST YORKSHIRE — M1

St Peter and St Leonard, Horbury

> **JUNCTIONS**
>
> **Wakefield/Ossett area**
>
> **Junction 40**
> The M1 crosses the A638, which connects Wakefield with the wool-textile manufacturing towns of the Spen valley.

famous hymn 'Onward Christian Soldiers' here in 1865, while he was curate.

Holy Trinity, Ossett ❹   At J40; 1m W

Holy Trinity, the parish church of Ossett, dominates the view from the M1 for several miles. A classic Victorian ecclesiastical blockbuster.

Holy Trinity   *Chimney*

Chimney, Ossett ❺   At J40; 1m W

This is the mill chimney of Walter Walker & Sons' textile factory *(to the right in the illustration above)*. The mill is no longer steam-powered, so the days of this prominent landmark may be numbered.

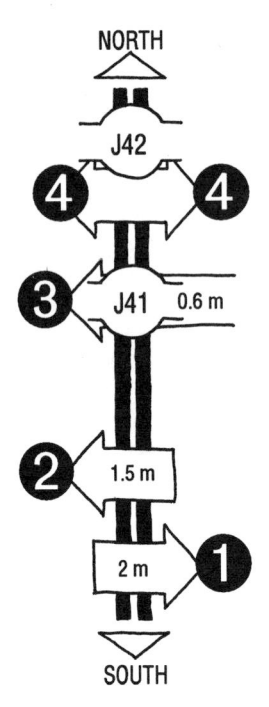

Wakefield skyline ① J40 to J41 ; 2m E

Wakefield is the county town of West Yorkshire. Before the rise of Leeds and Bradford it was the centre of the Yorkshire clothing industry, then came coal-mining. However, the city has never become a major industrial centre, always being overshadowed by Leeds and Bradford.

The main features of its skyline are:

Cathedral Much of the cathedral is over 500 years old with some parts over 700 years old, although until late in the nineteenth century it was simply the parish church. Fourteen bells are housed in its spire, which at 247 ft (75 m) is the highest in Yorkshire.

Town Hall The tower of the town hall is the second highest feature of the skyline. This was built in the 1870s to the design of T. E. Collcut, whose main claim to distinction seems to be that he also designed the Savoy Hotel in London.

County Hall Close to the Town Hall is the 1893 County Hall. The architects gave it an unusual dome-topped tower to compete with that of the Town Hall next door.

A little to the north of the town centre, you can see the spire of **St John's Church**. This is a beautifully proportioned late-eighteenth-century church which was built as the centre for a residential development: an early example of formal town planning — perhaps even the Milton Keynes of its day.

WEST YORKSHIRE — M1

Water tower, Dewsbury ②

1m N J40 ; 1.5m S J41 ; 1.5m W

A water tower serving the town of Dewsbury, which is just behind the skyline. Boring but essential.

St Michael, East Ardsley ③

At J41 ; 0.6m W

You could be forgiven for mistaking St Michael's for a castle, with its battlements and flag flying. In fact the building has housed nothing more sinister than the local congregation since its construction in 1881.

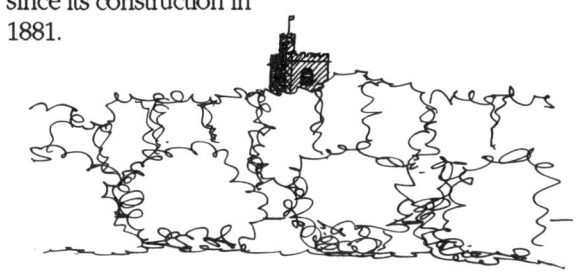

Rhubarb sheds ④

Several on each side of motorway for a few miles N of J41

The curious low black buildings in the fields are some of the few remaining rhubarb sheds. The crop is grown outside for two months and then moved into dark, heated sheds to be 'forced' before harvesting. Rhubarb develops fast in these sheds, and on quiet nights you can hear it creaking as it grows. Yorkshire was once the centre of the English rhubarb industry.

JUNCTIONS

Wakefield to M62

Junction 41
The M1 crosses the A650, which meanders in a half-hearted manner from Wakefield to Bradford via Morley.

Junction 42
The M1 crosses the M62, the main trans-Pennine route between Yorkshire and Lancashire.

M1 — WEST YORKSHIRE

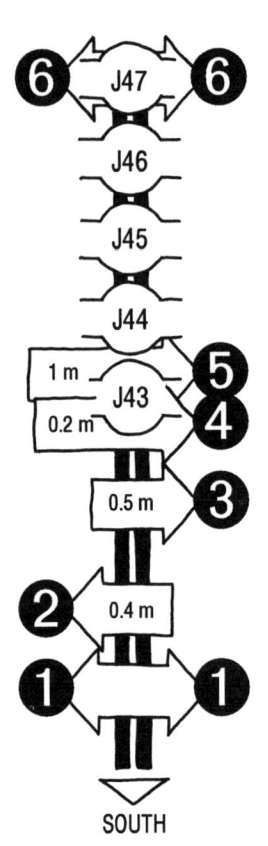

Mining cottages ❶ N of J42

The rows of cottages isolated on the hillsides are reminders of the Yorkshire coalfields. Barely a lifetime ago the view would have been dotted with pithead winding gear, but now it is often only the dwellings which show where the mines once were.

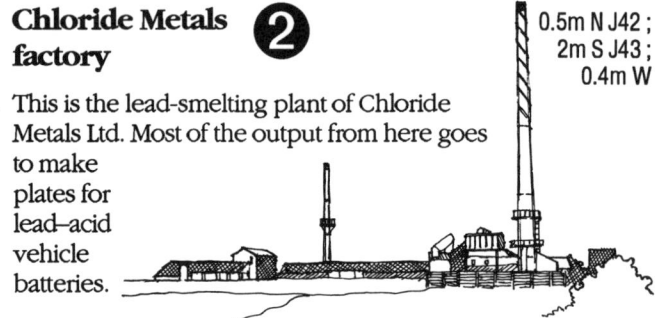

Chloride Metals factory ❷ 0.5m N J42; 2m S J43; 0.4m W

This is the lead-smelting plant of Chloride Metals Ltd. Most of the output from here goes to make plates for lead–acid vehicle batteries.

Tower, St George's Hospital ❸ 2m N J42; 1m S J43; 0.5m E

This building achieves prominence without grace, being a clumsy attempt at combining the functions of clock tower, water tower and chimney. The nearby village is Rothwell Haigh.

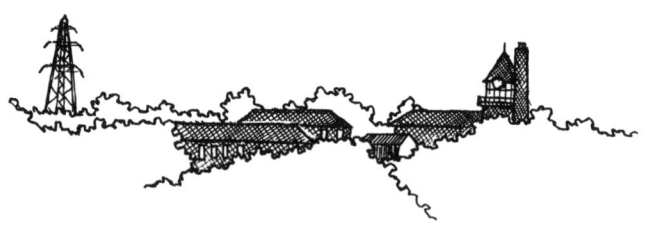

Rail depot lights, Rothwell ❹ At J43; 0.2 E

The lights on high pylons illuminate the Rothwell Railfreight and Containerbase depot. This is the main container-handling depot for West Yorkshire.

WEST YORKSHIRE — M1

Skelton Grange Power Station ⑤
At J43 ; 1m E

One of the most powerful coal-fired generating stations. Skelton Grange's four turbines annually supply 1,800 million units of electricity to the National Grid. The cooling water for the condensers in the prominent towers is drawn from the nearby River Aire.

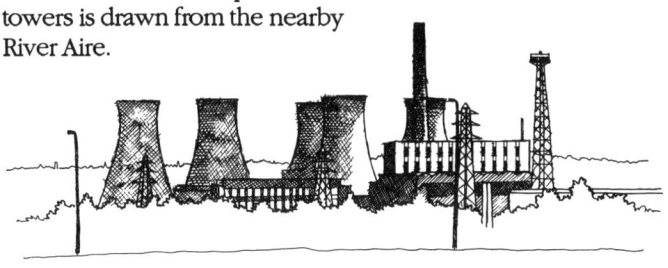

City of Leeds ⑥
At J47

A major manufacturing city which became very prosperous during Britain's industrial heyday. Leeds was the centre of the ready-made tailoring industry, as well as having many iron foundries and engineering works.

Manufacturing continues, but the city has also developed as a thriving financial and commercial centre. A recent addition is the Quarry Hill development, a large block of offices for the NHS Executive and Benefit Agency.

Tourism is being actively encouraged; a major project for the mid-1990s is the building of a new museum in the centre of the city to house the Royal Armouries Museum.

The M1 reached the outskirts of Leeds in 1972.

Population 445,000

JUNCTIONS

Leeds area

Junction 43
To Stourton, where there is a rail freight depot. Also A61 to Wakefield; A639 to Castleford and Pontefract.

Junction 44
To Middleton, where there is a light railway. Southbound exit only.

Junction 45
To Hunslet and Beeston. Northbound exit only.

Junction 46
A61 for Harrogate, Wetherby and York. Also Hunslet and Beeston (southbound).

Junction 47
A653 for Leeds city centre and Holbeck. At present the M1 finishes here; if you carry on you find yourself on the M621, which connects with the westbound M62.

Time changes the landscape

England is part of a small island which has been quite well populated for thousands of years, so very little of the landscape is still 'natural'. The vast forests which would have hidden much of the view a few hundred years ago were cut down to build wooden fighting ships or provide charcoal for the ironmasters. Huge areas of marshland have been drained and cultivated. Hills have been topped by castles, and rivers turned into both water highways and industrial drains. The change will continue, and the very existence of motorways is affecting the landscape. The out-of-town shopping malls and enormous blank-walled distribution sheds of the 1980s would never have appeared without motorways to carry the cars and trucks which they feed on.

These are a few of the times at which different features you can still see probably first appeared:

Earth hill forts

Over two thousand years old. If you see any unidentified lumps or ridges on hilltops, they can often be blamed on Bronze-age or Iron-age man.

Long straight stretches of road

Almost always built over Roman foundations. The Romans arrived in 55 BC and developed society greatly, but lost their grip about four hundred years later. They needed good roads over which to move their armies, and were unhampered by planning permissions or public enquiries. Much of the A1 follows the Roman routes exactly.

In contrast to the arrow-straight Roman roads, modern motorway surveyors deliberately introduce series of sweeping curves to keep drivers occupied, so that they are less likely to fall asleep at the wheel.

Castles

Surviving castles date from the Norman invasion of 1066 and onwards. The earliest are the 'motte and bailey' type, which was basically an earth mound with a strong wooden building on top. Many of the earth mounds remain.

Sandal Castle, West Yorkshire (M1)

Durable stone castles start at about the year 1100. Minor civil war between rival barons was a way of life in mediaeval times, so the castles were to protect the English against the English as much as anything else.

The position of a castle is most important, and those in the right places were constantly upgraded to keep up with the state of the art of war. Three hundred years after they were built, some early Norman castles stood up to the Wars of the Roses — a messy series of battles for the throne, carried on from 1455 to 1485 — and two centuries later were again doing serious business in the Civil War when Cromwell's troops fought the Royalists in 1642–45. And some still stand, although many were deliberately allowed to decay after the Civil War.

Lumley Castle, Co. Durham (A1)

As well as once-practical castles, many grand or elaborate buildings are called castles, often because they occupy a previous castle site.

Stately homes

From Elizabethan times onwards, the wealthy and noble of the country have indulged in a passion for building magnificent houses. Constructed regardless of cost and sometimes with money generated in what would now be considered very questionable ways, a number of these mansions can still be seen from the motorways.

Building stately homes, rather than ornamented castles, started around 1500 and carried on in one style or another until the end of the nineteenth century.

Hardwick Hall, Derbyshire (M1)

*Facing page:
RAF Wittering,
Cambridgeshire/
Northamptonshire (A1)*

TIME CHANGES THE LANDSCAPE

Mills and factories

Industrial buildings need raw materials and power, so they usually owe their position in the landscape to the availability of one or both. For example, windmills will naturally be erected in exposed positions in agricultural areas, just as coal-fired power stations are built close to coal and cooling water. Brickworks appear because the right sort of clay is nearby, and steel towns like Sheffield grow close to iron and coal mines.

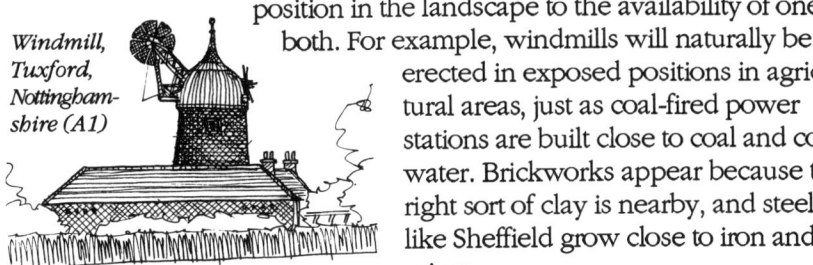

Windmill, Tuxford, Nottinghamshire (A1)

Most of the remains of windmills date from the early 1800s, while the big power stations along the Trent and on the Yorkshire coalfield are nearly all post-1950.

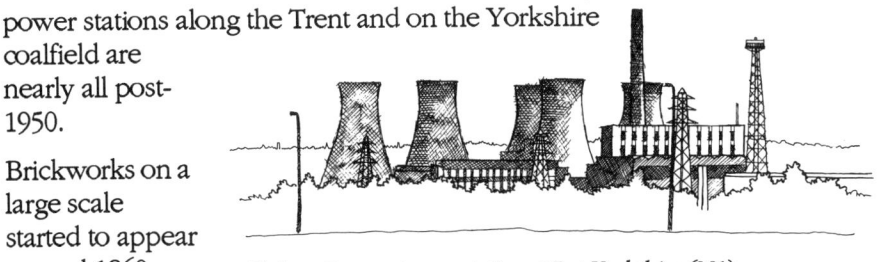

Brickworks on a large scale started to appear around 1860. Most of the other factories and works which are big enough to catch your eye from the motorway will be no older than that — monuments to the confidence and prosperity of Victorian industrialists.

Skelton Grange power station, West Yorkshire (M1)

We've seen plenty of evidence of the change in England's industry while we have been gathering material for this book. Coal mines, coking plants and steelworks have closed, while technology parks have opened. So many mill chimneys have been demolished that they are now almost a rarity.

Airfields

Most of the many airfields that lie close to the A1 were built during the period of rearmament in the late 1930s. They were originally positioned to protect industrial England from German attack.

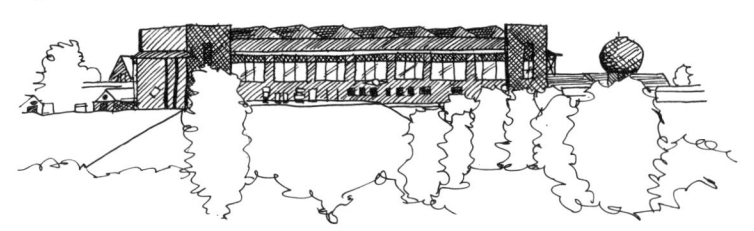

Canals and railways

Canal building started just after 1760 and continued with great energy for about eighty years. However, steam railways appeared on the scene in 1825; although not very efficient at first, they developed rapidly, soon covering the country with a comprehensive network. The canal boom had ended by 1840, when it was apparent that the railways could handle most of the traffic and deliver it more quickly.

Transmitting masts and aerials

The first prominent aerials appeared around 1900, but they have bred very rapidly since about 1960 with the growth of regional TV and radio. They come in many shapes and sizes. The tallest are the TV transmitters such as that at Emley Moor.

Smaller masts may be repeaters, to get TV signals into areas where reception would otherwise be poor, or VHF radio transmitters for a variety of private mobile radio users (PMRs) such as transport fleets and taxi services.

Cellnet and Vodaphone cell telephone aerials appear as sets of vertical rods — mounted sometimes on redundant chimneys, but usually on special masts of their own.

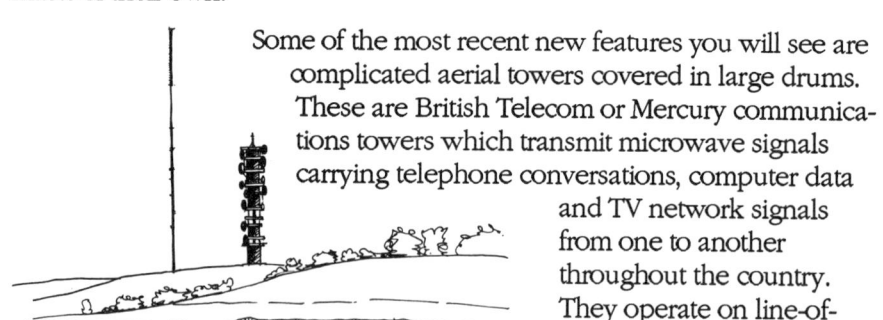

Some of the most recent new features you will see are complicated aerial towers covered in large drums. These are British Telecom or Mercury communications towers which transmit microwave signals carrying telephone conversations, computer data and TV network signals from one to another throughout the country. They operate on line-of-sight, so you will normally spot them on the tops of hills.

Morborne Hill, Cambridgeshire (A1)

Churches

The whole English landscape is punctuated with churches. Each time the road crests a hill, a couple more towers or steeples will usually appear on the skyline. There are far too many of them for us to refer to each one

TIME CHANGES THE LANDSCAPE

individually, so we have tended to write only of those which are particularly striking or have some extra claim on our interest.

Many of the churches you can see will date from the years between the Norman invasion of 1066 and the Black Death, a plague which swept through the land in 1348. This was a period of intense religious activity, and hundreds of town and village churches from the time still stand. Churches from this period were far more than simple houses of worship: they were usually the strongest buildings in

Diddington Church, Cambridgeshire (A1)

the community, and formed places of refuge and defence. The towers were used as lookout posts and beacons. Building almost stopped for many years after the plague, because the disease had killed vast numbers of the population and left the country short of able-bodied people of all types, including the craftsmen and builders.

Hanslope Church, Buckinghamshire (M1)

The prosperity founded on the industrial revolution resulted in intensive church building during Victorian times.

The churches of later centuries have usually followed the traditional styles, with a few notable exceptions such as the recent church of St Benedict near Northampton.

Towers, spires and steeples
Most churches have a tower; when this has a spire on top, the whole construction is called a steeple. The spire was considered to be a representation of the people's desire to be united with their creator. Unfortunately, many spires have been demolished by lightning or storms, and have been rebuilt in later styles.

There is huge variety in the size of spires. These start with small wooden 'fleche' spirelets rising from the centre of a low tower. Next are the much larger wooden-framed spires which can be covered with many different types of cladding — copper, lead and slate are common. Big stone spires were the most difficult to construct, and their great weight often proved more than a match for their foundations. However, there are still many standing which are a great tribute to the skills and labour of the workmen of the Middle Ages. Local communities become very protective about the quality of their particular steeple, and in our travels throughout the country we have encountered many which have been claimed to be the 'finest in the land'.

It is easy to see how cross-country horse races from one village to another became known as 'steeplechases' — the steeple was the obvious landmark for the riders to aim for. The name now lives on to describe any race over hedges.

Types and styles

Churches differ by far more than simply whether they have steeples or not. They are usually constructed from the local stone, which means that their colour can range from the almost-white of limestone to the near-black of weathered gritstone in the industrial towns. They can be quite small, like the mediaeval village churches, or positively oversized, like some of the Victorian blockbusters.

Generally, churches are aligned on an east–west axis, with the altar placed at the eastern end. This was originally done because it was believed that the worshippers within would then be facing Jerusalem. That was in the days when the world was assumed to be flat and maps were vague, but in spite of our improved knowledge of geography the tradition continues.

Almost all the church buildings you will spot from the motorways are for Church of England congregations. Nonconformist chapels do not stand out, as they rarely have towers or steeples. Roman Catholic churches can occasionally be seen, but they tend to be hidden in built-up areas: Roman Catholicism was suppressed in England until 1829, and its revival coincided with the industrial growth of Victorian times.

Clifford Roman Catholic Church (A1)

TIME CHANGES THE LANDSCAPE

Water towers

Water towers are a recurring feature of the landscape. They act as small reservoirs, ensuring that local communities receive a constant supply of water at a reasonable pressure. Water is pumped up into the tank at the top of the tower, from which it then flows by gravity to the taps of the users. The water towers are so prominent because the tank has to be higher than any of the outlets it supplies. Large users of water, such as factories and hospitals, frequently have their own water towers.

Water tower, Catterick, North Yorkshire (A1)

You will see water towers constructed from steel, concrete, stone, brick and even timber. Sometimes they are combined with chimneys, or disguised to look like castle turrets or mediaeval towers.

Water tower above Dewsbury, West Yorkshire (M1)

A1: List of Features

GEC factory	58	St Peter and St Paul,		Ferrybridge Power	
Dyrham Park	58	Great Casterton	71	Stations	86
Tower, Shenley		Woolfox Lodge airfield	72	TV mast, Emley Moor	86
Hospital	58	Greetham Inn	72	Fairburn Ings Nature	
Lodge, North Mymms		Ram Jam Inn	72	Reserve	86
Park	59	Cottesmore airfield	73	The Boot and Shoe Inn	87
Hatfield tunnel	59	Easton Park	73	Almshouses, Aberford	87
Hatfield	60	Christian Salvesen plant	74	Bowcliffe Hall	88
Stanborough Park and		Grantham	74	St Luke, St Edward,	
the River Lea	60	Harlaxton Manor	74	Clifford	88
The Frythe	60	Belvoir Castle	75	River Wharfe	89
Lockleys	61	Tower, Balderton		Wetherby	89
Knebworth House	61	Hospital	75	All Saints, Kirk Deighton	89
Stevenage	62	Newark-on-Trent	76	Lodge, Ribstone Hall	90
Lister Hospital	62	Staythorpe Power		The Bridge Inn	90
Letchworth	62	Station	76	Allerton Park	91
St Mary, Baldock	62	Sugar factory, Newark	77	Ornham's Hall	91
Fairfield Hospital	63	Winthorpe Hall	77	The Devil's Arrows	92
Aerial, Chicksands	63	River Trent	78	Boroughbridge	92
Biggleswade	63	Kelham Hall	78	The Hambleton Hills	93
Rivers Ivel and Great		St Wilfred, South		Dere Street	93
Ouse	63	Muskham	79	Leeming Lane	93
Sandy	64	Railway (London–		Dishforth airfield	94
Elevated silo, Sandy	64	Edinburgh)	79	Camp Hill	94
Tempsford Hall	64	High Marnham Power		Control tower, Leeming	
St Leonard, Southoe	64	Station	79	airfield	94
St Lawrence,		Windmill, Tuxford	79	Street House	95
Diddington	65	All Saints, Milton	80	Killerby Hall	95
Grafham Water dam	65	Bevercotes colliery	80	Yorkshire Dales	96
Buckden Palace	65	Gamston aerodrome	80	Catterick airfield	96
River Great Ouse	66	Chesterfield Canal	80	Richmond	96
Brampton Hotel	66	The Barracks	81	Scotch Corner Hotel	97
Huntingdon Research		St Mary and St Martin,		River Tees	98
Centre	66	Blyth	81	Darlington	98
Alconbury airfield	66	Harworth colliery	82	Walworth Castle	98
Brickworks, Yaxley	67	Tickhill	82	Fujitsu factory	99
Transmitter, Morborn		St John, Wadworth	82	Lime works, Ferryhill	99
Hill	67	Doncaster	83	Durham	99
Peterborough	67	Railway bridges,		Penshaw Monument	100
River Nene	68	Doncaster	83	Lumley Castle	101
Nene Valley Railway	68	Cusworth Hall	83	River Wear	101
The Haycock Inn	68	Robin Hood's Well	84	Chester-le-Street	101
Wittering airfield	69	Summer House Farm	84	Washington	102
Burghley House	69	River Aire; Aire and		Wearside	102
Wothorpe House	70	Calder Navigation	85	Tyneside	102
Stamford	70	Flour mills,		MetroCentre	103
Cement works, Ketton	71	Knottingley	85	On to Scotland	103

A1

The A1 was given its label in 1922, when the English road-numbering system was introduced, but it is still the Great North Road to many people. For centuries it was the only practical route connecting north-east England and Scotland with London. Much of the way it follows the military road which the Romans built for their legions almost two thousand years ago. Once the Romans had left, sections of the road became neglected and almost impassable for much of the year.

In the late eighteenth century things improved with the setting up of turnpike trusts, which allowed tolls to be charged in return for reasonable maintenance of the carriageway. Beside the road you can still occasionally see some of the little turnpike cottages where the tolls were collected.

Horse-drawn carriages could run long and fast over the turnpikes, and soon an elaborate system of stage coaches travelled the length of the Great North Road. Many of the inns where the teams of horses were changed at the end of each stage are still there, although in most cases you now need to leave the modern road and detour into the towns and villages to find them. The great days of the coaches were from about 1790 to 1835, by which time it was clear that the railways could move people over long distances far more efficiently. The use of the road then declined rapidly, and many of the more remote coaching inns went out of business.

Almost a hundred years later, the growth of popular motoring put the traffic back on the Great North Road. Unfortunately, it was not really up to the job; even in the 1930s, traffic in the towns was a problem. The first by-pass, around Barnet, was built then, but overall improvement was slow. Until the 1960s the A1 passed through the centres of most of the towns and villages along its way, and there were even railway level-crossings on it. During the 1960s and 1970s, many by-passes were built and all the busiest parts were gradually converted to dual carriageways. Now the road is changing again as large sections are upgraded to motorway standard.

This book covers the A1 near its junction with the M25, just north of London, to the outskirts of Newcastle, a distance of about 265 miles. Virtually all of this will be upgraded to motorway standard by the end of the 1990s.

This constant programme of improvement means that re-routing of some stretches of the road occurs from time to time, sometimes making certain features more difficult to spot, but sometimes bringing others into clearer view.

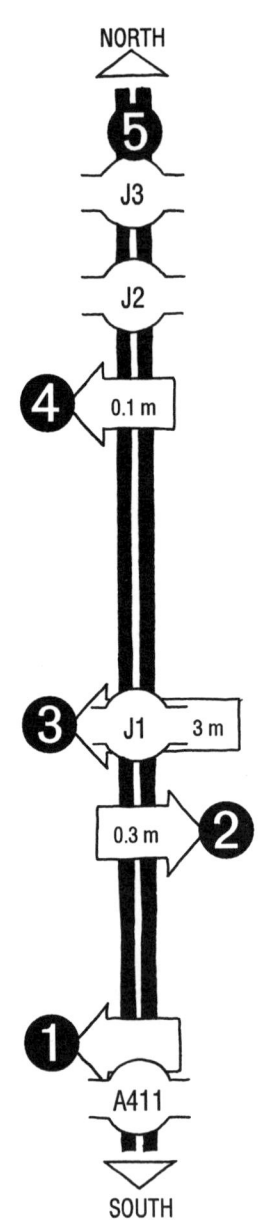

We start at Stirling Corner, the junction of the A1 with the A411 on the southern edge of Borehamwood.

GEC factory ❶   0.5m N Stirling Corner ; 3m S J1 ; adj. W

It's possible that the last red light that held up your journey came from here — this is the home of GEC Alsthom Traffic Control Automation. Also in Borehamwood is GEC Alsthom Signalling, who design and make railway signalling equipment.

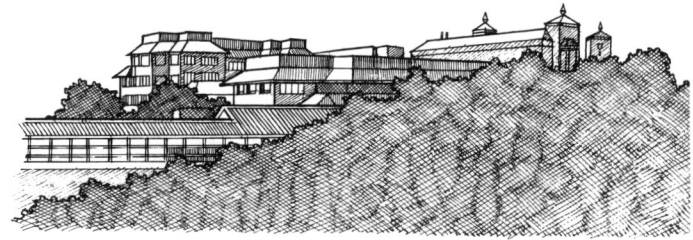

Dyrham Park ❷   2.5m N Stirling Corner ; 1m S J1 ; 0.3m E

Dyrham House stands in 170 acres of parkland. It can just be glimpsed through the trees. The area derives its name from the Derham family, who owned the land in the early fourteenth century. The present house dates from around 1800. The park has had a host of owners, including John Trotter, an army contractor who made a fortune through the Napoleonic Wars. Trotter is remembered mainly for founding the Soho Bazaar, which opened in 1816 to enable widows and daughters of army officers to sell their craftwork — often a vital source of income for them in the days before the welfare state.

The parkland is now a golf course.

Tower, Shenley Hospital ❸   At J1 ; 3m W

The services tower at Shenley Hospital. See M1, page 11, for more details.

HERTFORDSHIRE — A1

Lodge, North Mymms Park ④   3m N J1 ; 1m S J2 ; 0.1m W

You can see the ornate Octagon Lodge at the eastern edge of North Mymms Park. This has been a fine estate since Elizabethan times. North Mymms House, one of the best surviving late-Elizabethan residences, hides in the trees about half a mile away behind the lodge. The lodge was completely renovated in 1989.

Hatfield tunnel ⑤   0.5m N J3 ; 1m S J4

The A1(M) now dives through a huge tunnel between the town of Hatfield to the east and the British Aerospace factory and airfield to the west. The tunnel was opened by the Duke of Kent in 1986, as part of a £30 million Department of Transport development. The land over the tunnel has now been developed into Hatfield Park Plaza, which includes the Galleria shopping mall. Conceived during the boom of the 1980s, this project ran into financial difficulties in the early 1990s and is unlikely to be fully developed, particularly now that the entire British Aerospace factory is to close.

JUNCTIONS

Potters Bar/ Hatfield area

A411
Watford and Barnet (Stirling Corner).

Junction 1
Bignells Corner, the junction with the M25, the London orbital motorway.

Junction 2
A1001 to Hatfield

Junction 3
A414 St Albans

A1 — HERTFORDSHIRE

Hatfield ①
J2 to J4 ; adjacent E

Originally a village based around Hatfield Palace, Hatfield itself was greatly extended in the 1920s and 1930s as part of the series of new towns and garden cities which developed between the A1 and the railway. The railway runs almost parallel to the road from London to just north of Stevenage.

Stanborough Park and the River Lea ②
0.5m N J4 ; 3.25m S J6 ; adj. E

Just north of the Hatfield tunnel, the A1(M) crosses the River Lea. This rises in Luton and flows around Hertford before turning south to enter the Thames in the East End of London, near the Blackwall Tunnel. During its course it changes its spelling from Lea to Lee and back again several times.

Look for the large fountain in Stanborough Park, beside the motorway to the east. The River Lea runs through the park.

The Frythe ③
3m N J4 ; 0.75m S J6 ; 0.2m W

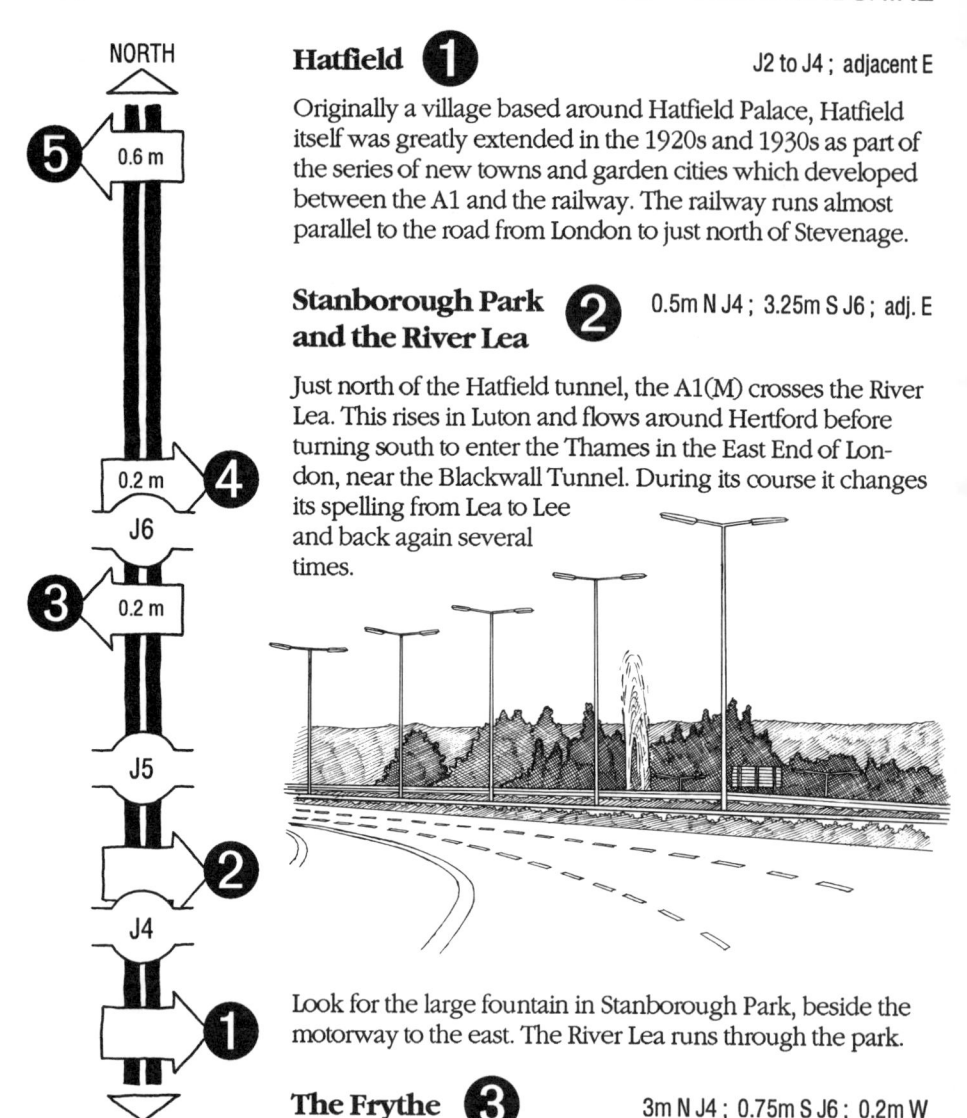

The Frythe is the big Tudor-style manor house which is just visible through the trees on the west of the road. It was built in 1846, but the Wilshere family, who own the manor, have lived on the site since the late fourteenth century.

On the other side of the road are the outskirts of Welwyn Garden City. Welwyn Garden City was started in 1920, to the plan of Sir Ebenezer Howard (see Letchworth, page 62).

HERTFORDSHIRE — A1

Lockleys ④   0.25m N J6 ; 4.25m S J7 ; 0.2m E

Lockleys was built in 1717 by Edward Searle, a wealthy merchant. The handsome brick-built house is now a private school called Sherrardswood. There are the remains of several Roman buildings in the grounds, including a suite of baths, over which the A1(M) passes. The bathhouse was preserved by encasing it in a concrete vault when the motorway was constructed.

Knebworth House ⑤   3.5m N J6 ; 1m S J7 ; 0.6m W

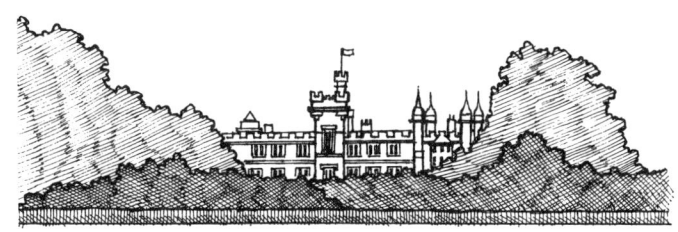

> **JUNCTIONS**
>
> **Welwyn Garden City area**
>
> **Junction 4**
> Hatfield, Welwyn Garden City and A414 to Hertford
>
> **Junction 5**
> Access from Welwyn Garden City onto the northbound carriageway only
>
> **Junction 6**
> B1000 Welwyn Garden City

The Knebworth you now see from the A1(M) is an enormous dog's breakfast of a house, most of which was constructed in the nineteenth century. Much of the work was commissioned by Sir Edward Bulwer-Lytton, a highly successful novelist and statesman. He produced a large number of romantic and historical novels which were critically reviled but which became best-sellers — a sort of Victorian Jeffrey Archer.

Various architects, including Sir Edwin Lutyens of Cenotaph fame, have had a fist in putting together the rambling pile that is Knebworth House.

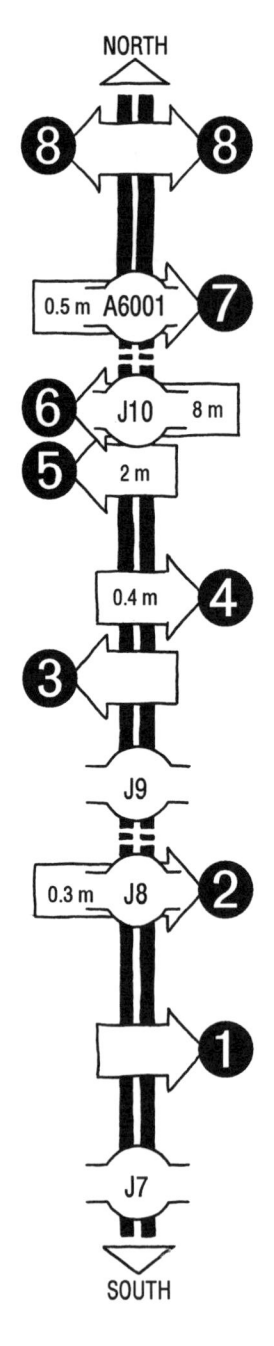

A1 — HERTFORDSHIRE

Stevenage ①
J7 to J8 ; adjacent E

The factories and warehouses on the right of the A1(M) are in the industrial estates of Stevenage, which lie between the road and the town centre. Stevenage was a small town until the late 1940s, when it was greatly expanded during the first wave of postwar enthusiasm for new-town development.

Lister Hospital ②
At J8 ; 0.3m E

The main general hospital for the area, providing acute, accident and emergency services. Operated by the North Hertfordshire NHS Trust.

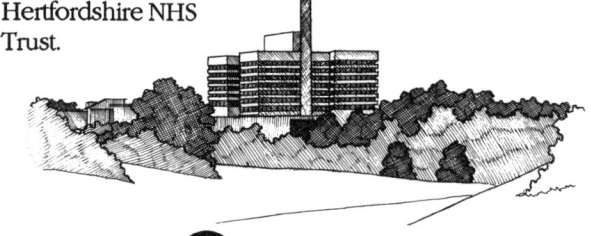

Letchworth ③
1m N J9 ; 2 m S J10 ; adjacent W

Letchworth, just to the west of the A1(M), was the first of the English garden cities. It was founded in 1903, under the inspiration of Sir Ebenezer Howard, a visionary town planner who was determined to improve on the the chaotic way towns and cities had been allowed to grow during the industrial revolution.

The garden-city idea was to provide fairly open development, with farmland and recreational areas being important features of the town. Letchworth was successful, and was followed in 1920 by the building of Welwyn Garden City a few miles further south.

St Mary, Baldock ④
1.75m N J9 ;
1.75m S J10 ;
0.4m E

The church of St Mary dates from the early 1300s. The little 'spike' spire is typical of Hertfordshire, but is unusual in being mounted on a cylindrical 'lantern', rather than rising directly from the tower. In contrast, on the opposite side of the road is the modern industrial area of Letchworth.

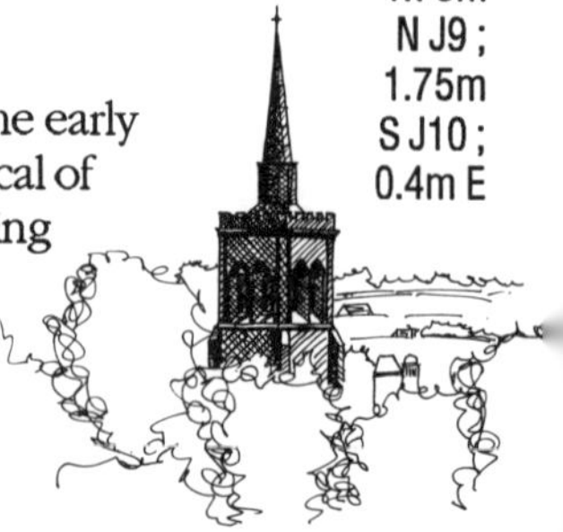

BEDFORDSHIRE — A1

Fairfield Hospital ⑤   3m N J9 ; 0.5m S J10 ; 2m W

Fairfield Hospital is a couple of miles to the west of the road. You can see its towers with their rather exotic domes and pinnacles. This is a huge psychiatric hospital run by the North West Thames Health Authority. Building began in 1857, and many additions were made during the next three decades. The architect was George Fowler Jones, of York.

Aerial, Chicksands ⑥   At J10 ; 8m W

If the weather is clear, you will be able to spot this large steel construction from the A1, appearing like the frame of an unfinished building. This is the vast radio aerial at RAF Chicksands. Each of the uprights is 120 ft (37 m) high, and they stand in a circle which is nearly a quarter of a mile round, although it is hard to get a sense of the scale because it is almost eight miles from the road. The Chicksands aerial is operated by the United States Air Force for military communication.

Biggleswade ⑦   At A6001 ; 0.5m E

Biggleswade was an important staging post on the old Great North Road, and there are a number of coaching inns in the town. The A1 ran through the centre until the 1960s.

Rivers Ivel and Great Ouse ⑧   1.5m N A6001 to A14

Just outside the town of Biggleswade, the A1 crosses the River Ivel, which runs alongside the road until it meets the Great Ouse, a couple of miles north of the village of Sandy. The A1 follows the valley of the Great Ouse until Brampton, just outside Huntingdon. Here the river continues east to meander across East Anglia, eventually to enter the sea at the Wash, while the road leaves the flat levels of Bedfordshire and climbs up to Alconbury.

JUNCTIONS

Stevenage/ Letchworth area

Junction 7
A602 Stevenage (South)

Junction 8
A602 Stevenage (North) and Hitchin

Junction 9
A6141 Letchworth and Baldock

Junction 10
A507 Baldock

A6001
Biggleswade

A1 — BEDFORDSHIRE

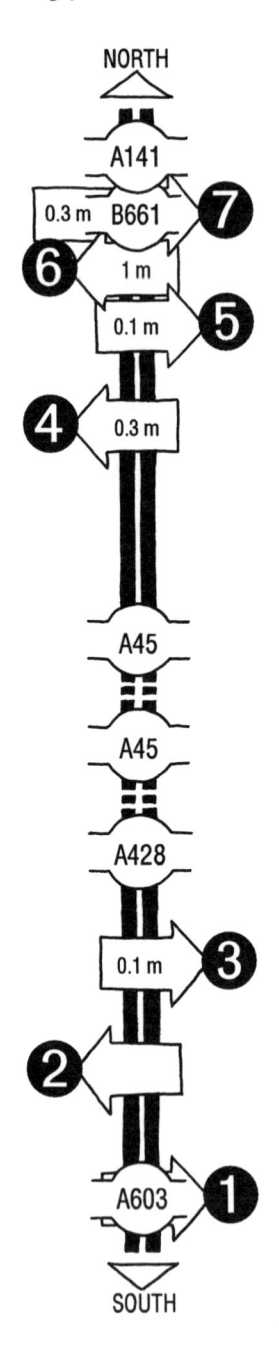

Sandy ❶ *At A603 ; adjacent E*

The only thing of note is the collection of factories on the east side of the town near the station: RKB Precision Products; Lion Aluminium; Kemira Fertilisers; Rega Domestic Products.

Elevated silo, Sandy ❷ *1.75m N A603 ; 2.5m S A428 ; adjacent W*

This elevated silo is above the nursery of C Zwetsloots and Sons. It contains woodchippings which are burned to provide heating for the nursery greenhouses, in which Zwetsloots grow vast numbers of cut flowers for supply to wholesalers.

Tempsford Hall ❸ *3m N A603 ; 1.25m S A428 ; 0.1m E*

A large house just visible through the trees. Elizabethan in style, it was built in 1898.

St Leonard, Southoe ❹ *2m N A45 ; 2m S B661 ; 0.3m W*

St Leonard's Church is mainly in the English Perpendicular style of the fifteenth century, although parts of it date from Norman times.

CAMBRIDGESHIRE — A1

St Lawrence, Diddington ⑤
3m N A45 ; 1m S B661 ; 0.1m E

St Lawrence, Diddington, stands alone just beside the road. It is a Tudor building, built of brick and stone during the reign of Henry VIII.

Grafham Water dam ⑥
3.5m N A45 ; 0.5m S B661 ; 1m W

The low dam of Grafham Water is just visible. This is part of Anglian Water's extensive modern reservoir system which is designed to meet the needs of towns from Milton Keynes to Peterborough. The dam itself is just over a mile long. Work began in 1961 and was completed in 1966. The area of the reservoir is 1570 acres; the maximum depth is 70 ft (21 m).

Buckden Palace ⑦
At B661 ; 0.3m E

The four turrets of the Great Tower of Buckden Palace are easily visible from the A1 as it by-passes the town. The tower is the chief remaining feature of the old fortified palace, which was the home of the bishops of Lincoln from 1178 to 1843. Once the bishops had moved to Lincoln itself, much of the building was demolished. Even so, the remains are quite extensive. They now serve as a Roman Catholic centre for teaching and retreat.

The fifteenth-century steeple of St Mary's Church is close to the tower.

JUNCTIONS

St Neots area

A603
Sandy and Bedford

A428
Bedford

A45 (east)
Cambridge and **B1428** St Neots

A45 (west)
Wellingborough and **B1048** St Neots

B661
Grafham Water and Buckden

A141
Brampton

A1 — CAMBRIDGESHIRE

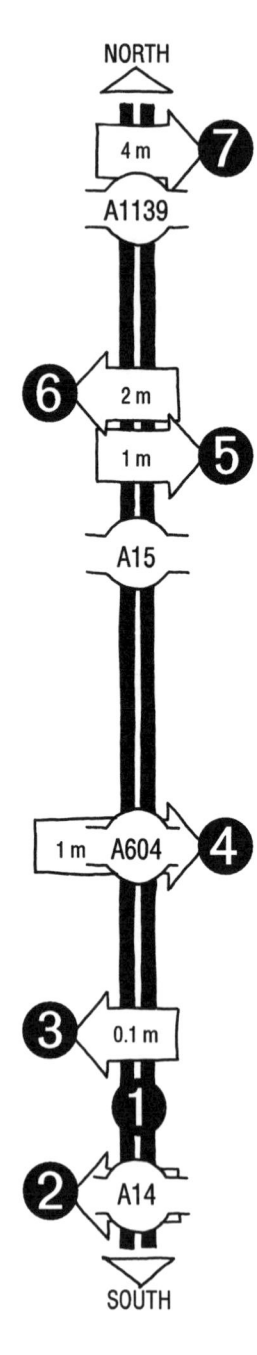

River Great Ouse ①

Going north, at Brampton the A1 leaves the valley of the Great Ouse — see page 63 for more details.

Brampton Hotel ②   At A14; adjacent W

An inn has stood at the crossroads here for hundreds of years, being altered and rebuilt from time to time. However, the recent additions represent a high point in architectural insensitivity. It has only recently been dignified by being called a hotel — many older travellers will still think of it by its familiar name of the 'Brampton Hut'.

Huntingdon Research Centre ③   1.5m N A14; 1.75m S A604; 0.1m W

The HRC is a completely independent establishment which tests the safety and environmental effects of drugs, pharmaceuticals, industrial chemicals and veterinary products. The centre has been operating for over 30 years and employs 950 people. It is the largest single research establishment of this type in the world.

Owing to the nature of some of the work carried out there, the HRC has occasionally been the focus of animal-rights protests.

Alconbury airfield ④   At A604; 1m E

Alconbury started its life in 1938, as a grass airfield for bombers. During the war it was a base for both British and American aircraft, including Halifaxes, Mosquitos and Liberators. The airfield was taken over by the USAF in 1953 and developed as a base for very high-flying reconnaissance aircraft. It continues to be an important US base, contributing to NATO defences.

CAMBRIDGESHIRE — A1

Brickworks, Yaxley ⑤

1m N A15 ; 2.5m S A1139 ; 1m E

The chimneys of large brickworks near Yaxley are easily spotted from the road. This is typical of a number of such works in the area.

Transmitter, Morborn Hill ⑥

1.5m N A15 ; 2m S A1139 ; 2m W

The tall thin stayed mast is the BBC's Peterborough transmitter, 502 ft (153 m) high. It transmits Radios 1, 2, 3 & 4 (40 kW) and Radio Cambridgeshire, all on FM.

Peterborough ⑦

A1139 to A605 ; 4m E

Peterborough grew up around a 7th-century Saxon monastery. The cathedral was rebuilt after the Conquest of 1066 and is now one of the most important Norman buildings in England.

The prosperity of modern Peterborough owes much to the manufacture of bricks — 'Flettons' got their name from a village nearby — and to sugar processing, but great efforts are being made to attract other industries to the area. The modern developments beside the A1, close to the East of England Showground, typify this effort.

JUNCTIONS

Huntingdon/ Peterborough area

A14 (old A604)
Kettering and Brampton

A604 (old A14)
Huntingdon and Cambridge

A15
Yaxley and Peterborough
(Norman Cross)

A1139
Peterborough

A1 — CAMBRIDGESHIRE

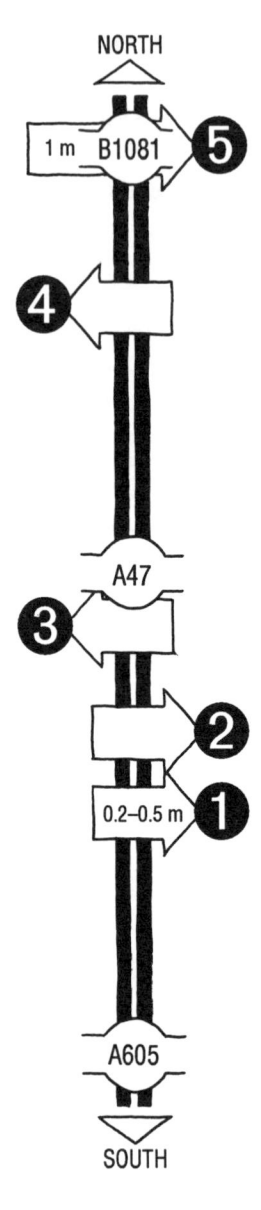

River Nene ①
A605 to A47 ; 0.2–0.5m E

Pleasure boats can be seen on the River Nene, alongside the A1. This was once an important working waterway; to the west it is navigable as far as Northampton, where the Grand Union Canal joins it. To the east, boats may travel to Peterborough and on across East Anglia to the Wash.

The river's name is pronounced 'Neen' at the Peterborough end and 'Nenn' at the Northampton end.

Nene Valley Railway ②
3m N A605 ; 1.5m S A47 ; adj. E

This is a preserved steam railway with more than seven miles of track. From its headquarters at the old Wansford station, close to the A1, the lines run right into the centre of Peterborough. The railway has an international flavour, with historic rolling stock from many European countries. Steam trains run on most weekends throughout the year and also at other times during peak holiday periods.

The Haycock Inn ③
4m N A605 ; 0.5m S A47 ; adj. W

The Haycock Inn at Wansford is a fine old coaching inn which the main road has by-passed for many years. Its full title is 'The Haycock Inn at Wansford-in-England'. Legend has it that during a flood in the dim and distant past, a local character was washed down the River Nene while soundly asleep on a haycock. Awaking among strangers many parishes downstream, he was asked from whence he came. 'Why, from Wansford, in England', he replied. The name has stuck.

CAMBRIDGESHIRE — A1

Wittering airfield ④   2.5m N A47 ; 1.5m S B1081 ; adj. W

RAF Wittering was opened during the First World War, when it was known as Stamford. It was not called Wittering until 1924. Between the wars it was the home of the RAF Central Flying School for many years. In the Second World War, a huge variety of aircraft, both British and American, used Witttering. For some time it was also the base of the flight which evaluated captured enemy planes, so you might have seen Heinkels, Messerschmitts and Focke-Wulfs being tested here.

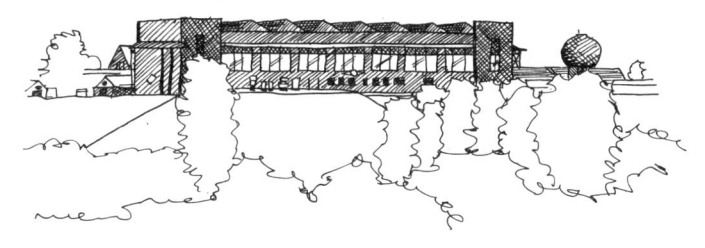

JUNCTIONS

Peter-borough/Stamford area

A605
Oundle and Peterborough

A47
Leicester and Peterborough (and eventually Great Yarmouth)

B1081
Stamford

Since 1970, RAF Wittering has served as the main base for training Harrier pilots.

Burghley House ⑤   At B1081 ; 1m E

You can only see the edge of the deer park around Burghley — the house itself remains tantalisingly out of sight.

Burghley is well worth making a stop for. It is a magnificent Elizabethan house which has been mercifully little altered outside since William Cecil, the first Lord Burghley, built it almost 450 years ago. It is still the home of the Cecil family, but many of the rooms are open to visitors.

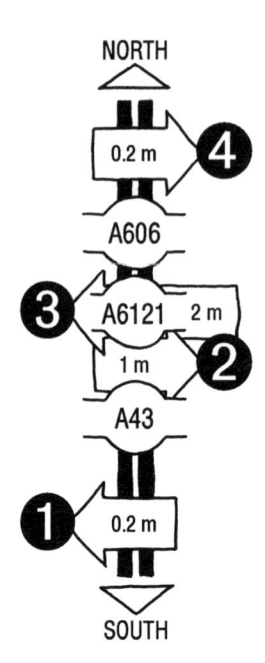

A1 — CAMBRIDGESHIRE

Wothorpe House ①   1m N B1081 ; 1m S A6121 ; 0.2m W

The four towers are the remains of a large and gracious lodge which was built for Lord Burghley's son, Thomas Cecil. He would apparently settle here when domestic pressures at Burghley House got too much for him. Burghley is only a mile or so away, on the other side of the A1.

Thomas Cecil became Earl of Exeter. His career was not as notable as his father's, although he did have the distinction of sailing with the fleet that beat the Spanish Armada in 1588.

Stamford ②   A43 to A606 ; 1m E

Over a thousand years ago, Stamford was one of the centres from which the Danes ruled. Throughout the Middle Ages it was an important religious centre, and it is still rich in mediaeval churches. In the eighteenth and nineteenth centuries it was a busy staging post for coaches on their way to Leeds, Edinburgh, York, Leicester and Cambridge.

Because the main railway line by-passed Stamford, the town has remained almost untouched by the industrial revolution. The world's heaviest man, Daniel Lambert, died while passing through Stamford in 1809, and is buried here. In his 'prime' he weighed almost 53 stones (742 lb, or 337 kg).

The Stamford skyline: from left to right are the churches of All Saints, St John the Baptist, St Michael and St Mary.

LEICESTERSHIRE — A1   71

Cement works, Ketton ③   At A6121 ; 2m W

The plant visible to the west of Stamford is the Castle Cement Works, near the village of Ketton. This is beside a huge quarry which has been the source of limestone for hundreds of years.

JUNCTIONS
Stamford area
A43 Stamford and Corby (limited access)
A6121 Stamford
A606 Stamford and Oakham

As well as the relatively low-quality stone which is used on a vast scale for cement and fertilizer manufacture, a small amount of the famous high-grade Ketton limestone is still quarried here. This material has long been thought of as one of the best building stones in the country — much of Cambridge was constructed from it — but it is now almost worked out. What little remains is normally reserved for restoration work.

St Peter and St Paul, Great Casterton ④   0.75m N A606 ; 11m S A151 ; 0.2m E

From the A1 you get a really good view of the tower of the church of St Peter and St Paul, with its intricate belfry window, four handsome pinnacles, and prominent weathercock.

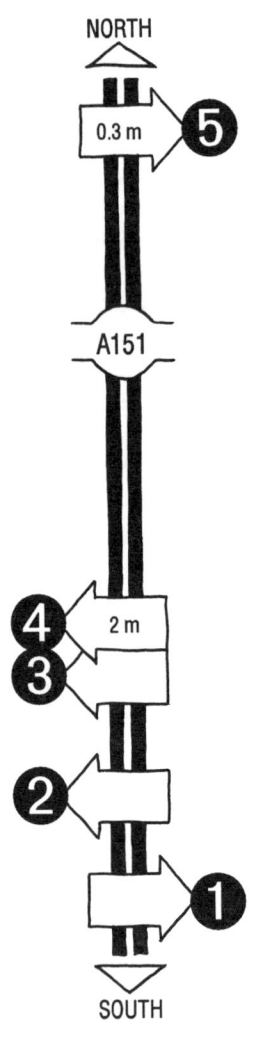

A1 — LEICESTERSHIRE

Woolfox Lodge airfield ❶
4.5m N A606; 7.25m S A151; adjacent E

The A1 runs right alongside the remnants of Woolfox Lodge airfield. Closed in 1966 and now back in agricultural use, this was originally a relief landing ground for nearby Cottesmore (see page 73). It housed a variety of units during the Second World War, and also served as a German POW camp.

Greetham Inn ❷
6m N A606; 5.75m S A151; adj. W

This was once a well-known coaching inn which was run by the same family that had the famous Haycock Inn at Wansford, a dozen miles to the south.

Ram Jam Inn ❸
6.75m N A606; 5m S A151; adj. W

Another of the coaching inns along the Great North Road, the Ram Jam is said to be named after a particularly vicious alcoholic drink which could be bought only here two hundred or more years ago. The host at the time had served in India, and named his special concoction after the name for an Indian servant, Ram Jan.

Apart from its coaching connections, the inn has had a colourful career, being a great site for bare-knuckle fighting in the 19th century, and the scene of many memorable drinking sessions by aircrew from nearby RAF and USAF stations during the Second World War.

LINCOLNSHIRE — A1

Cottesmore airfield ④   7m N A606 ; 4.75m S A151 ; 2m W

JUNCTIONS

Colsterworth area

A151
Corby Glen and Bourne

Cottesmore was officially opened in 1938, during the great pre-war expansion of the RAF. After a few years as an operational training base for bomber crews, it was transferred to American control in 1943. Cottesmore was very active throughout the Second World War; as well as participating in the thousand-bomber raids, planes towed gliders from here, carrying US paratroops to landings in Normandy on D-Day, and later at Arnhem.

After the war, Cottesmore eventually became a V-bomber base until such aircraft were phased out. It is now the home of the Tri-National Tornado Training Establishment (TTTE), responsible for training British, Italian and German crews to fly Tornados.

Easton Park ⑤   2m N A151 ; 5.5m S A607 ; 0.3m E

This group of buildings is what remains of Easton Park, a stately home and gardens, once the seat of the Cholmeley family. This must have been a spectacular place, with seven terraces of the French-style formal gardens cascading down the hillside. The house has long since been demolished, but various buildings remain, most outstanding of which is the 'Gothick' lodge.

A1 — LINCOLNSHIRE

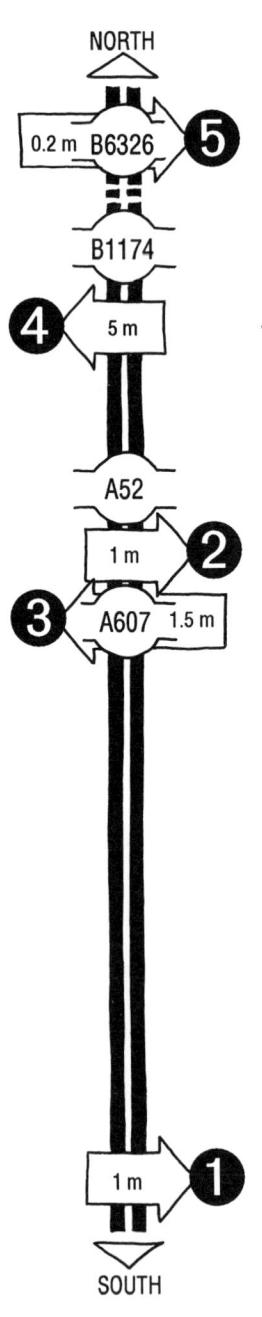

Christian Salvesen plant ❶
2m N A151 ; 5.5m S A607 ; 1m E

The large industrial buildings at the top of the ridge above Easton is a cold store belonging to the Christian Salvesen company. It is claimed to be the largest such store in Europe, but in spite of our repeated requests for information, the company has not produced any supporting facts and figures.

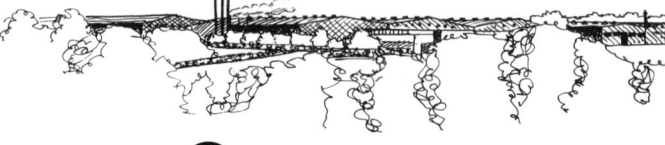

Grantham ❷
A607 to A52 ; 1m E

Grantham, birthplace of Margaret, Lady Thatcher, has frequently been cited in the popular press as the most boring town in England. While researching this book, we found little to contradict this. However, the staff of the Information Office in the town were extremely helpful and proved to be an excellent source of information about attractions in the surrounding countryside.

Harlaxton Manor ❸
At A607 ; 1.5m W

This grand and elaborate house is near the bottom of the line of hills running south-west from Grantham. In spite of its size, it is surprisingly easy to miss; you get the best view when you look south-west as the A1 climbs north past the town (just south of the A52 junction).

NOTTINGHAMSHIRE — A1

Building began in 1831, for George de Ligne Gregory, apparently to house his increasing art collection and to rival recent work at nearby Belvoir Castle. Harlaxton has a style of its own — unrestrained would be a good word. The architect of the exterior was Anthony Salvin, who also worked on extensions to the Tower of London and Windsor Castle. The stone came from the Ketton limestone quarry which is visible from the road just outside Stamford (see page 71).

Nowadays Harlaxton is the European outpost of the University of Evansville, Indiana. Each year 200 American students come here for courses in British and European studies.

Belvoir Castle ④   A52 to 3m N B1174 ; 5m S B6326 ; 5m W

The many turrets of Belvoir Castle can sometimes be hard to separate from the trees on the hillside surrounding it. The families of the Dukes of Rutland have lived in a castle on this site since one of their forebears came to England as a standard-bearer with William the Conqueror's adventure tour in 1066.

The present castle was built in early Victorian times, after its predecessor had been destroyed by fire. It is now the scene of jousting tournaments during the summer, and the gardens and much of the splendid interior are open to the public.

Belvoir overlooks the Vale of Belvoir, and gets its name from the Old French 'bel voir', meaning beautiful view. However, with typical English perversity, it is always pronounced 'beever'.

Tower, Balderton Hospital ⑤   At B6326 ; 0.2m E

The services tower of Balderton Hospital is a prominent feature of this section of the road. Balderton is a North Nottinghamshire Health Authority mental hospital.

JUNCTIONS
Grantham area
A607 Grantham
A52 Grantham, Boston and Nottingham
B1174 Grantham
B6326 Newark

A1 — NOTTINGHAMSHIRE

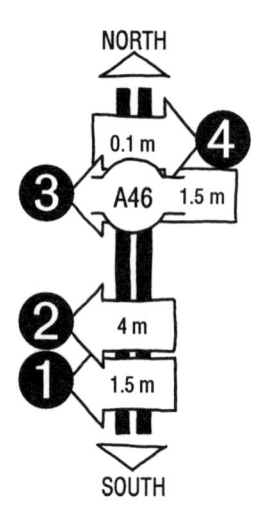

Newark-on-Trent ①   B6326 to A46 ; 1.5m W

Newark is a Norman town, having been built on land which was given by William the Conqueror to the Bishop of Lincoln. Its position near the River Trent has helped it to prosper through the centuries from the wool trade, agriculture and engineering.

St Mary Magdalene

Newark Castle

Two buildings stand out on the skyline:

St Mary Magdalene The pride of the town, and one of the best parish churches in the country. Henry III is recorded to have given six oaks from Sherwood Forest towards the building work. The steeple, formed from a tower surmounted by an octagonal spire, rises to 237 ft (72 m).

Newark Castle Started by Alexander, Bishop of Lincoln about 1133. It is sited on cliffs 170 ft (50 m) above the River Devon, which joins the Trent about a mile to the north of the town.

Newark Castle has unfortunate connotations for the British monarchy. King John, of Magna Carta fame, died here in 1216. He had spent much of his reign in conflict with the Pope and was not the most popular of monarchs: there is a theory that he was poisoned by local monks.

During the Civil War Newark was a Royalist stronghold, and after a series of sieges Charles I was captured here in 1646. The castle received a severe battering while under siege, and Oliver Cromwell ordered that it should be allowed to become derelict, so now only a few walls remain.

Staythorpe Power Station ②   2.5m N B6326 ; 1.25m S A46 ; 4m W

About four miles to the west of the road, you can see the chimneys of National Power's Staythorpe generating station. Staythorpe is a relatively small plant (360 megawatts); it has no cooling towers, because enough cooling water can be drawn from the River Trent, which runs alongside.

NOTTINGHAMSHIRE — A1

Staythorpe Power Station

JUNCTIONS
Newark area
A46 Newark, Leicester and Lincoln, and **A17** Sleaford

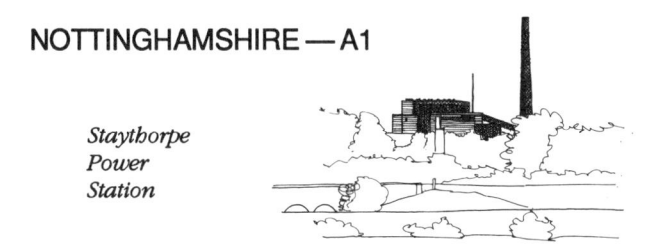

Sugar factory, Newark ❸ At A46 ; 1.5m W

Operated by British Sugar plc, this is one of the most modern sugar factories in Europe. Raw beet from local farms goes in and a variety of refined products comes out, including granulated sugar for the popular Silver Spoon packets which you find stacked up in the supermarkets. As well as food for human consumption, the factory can make 7,000 tonnes of sugar beet pellets for animal feed each day. All the production figures are enormous: the factory processes over 850,000 tonnes of beet during the four-month annual season; at the busiest times this can involve 550 lorry-loads a day. The main concrete silos, which you can clearly see from the road, each hold 12,000 tonnes

Winthorpe Hall ❹ 0.5m N A46 ; 2m S B6325 ; 0.1m E

This is an imposing house in the Palladian style, which overlooks the Trent valley. It dates from about 1761, and was built for Dr Robert Taylor. Taylor was a Newark doctor whose life was changed when he was called to treat the Earl of Burlington, who was staying at Belvoir Castle (see page 75). Burlington was so impressed with Taylor that he helped him to set up an extensive practice in London, and he eventually became physician to George II. Unfortunately, Taylor died before the hall was completed, and he never lived here. The grounds have gradually been eaten away by housing and the hall is now used as a nursing home.

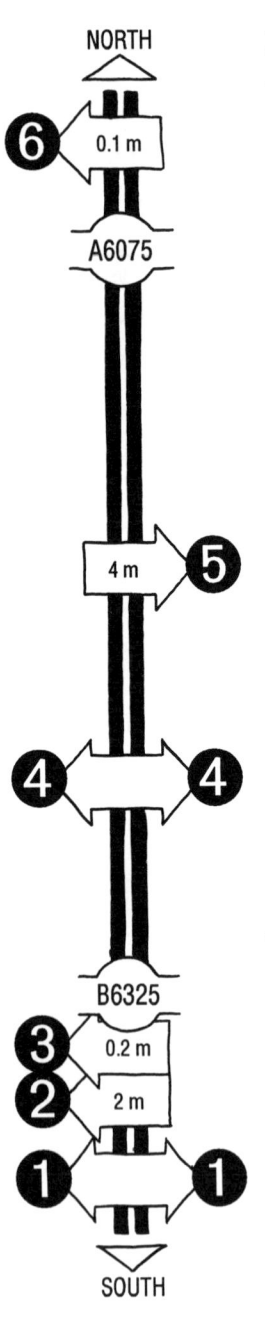

River Trent ① 0.75m N A46; 1.75m S B6325; crosses

The A1 crosses the River Trent (see page 27 for more details) almost directly north of Newark. This stretch of the river is known as the Winthorpe Rack. There are sand and gravel pits all along it, some of which can be seen on the west side of the road. The Trent runs west–east, and is tidal just 4 miles downstream from here, 53 miles from where it flows into the River Humber.

Kelham Hall ② 1.5m N A46; 1m S B6325; 2m W

Kelham Hall shows itself as a mixture of roofs, pinnacles, chimneys and turrets rising above the trees to the west of the A1. The original hall was burned down in 1857 while Sir George Gilbert Scott (see also Doncaster, page 83) was organising alterations to it. The owner, John Manners-Sutton, who was MP for Newark, then let Scott loose on designing a replacement. He produced this red-brick Victorian gothic wonder, but unfortunately the project ran over budget and was never totally completed. Because of the fire in the old house, as little timber as possible was used in the construction of the new one, to avoid a similar fate. Here, wood is to be found only in the roof and the banisters.

For most of this century Kelham Hall was a monastery, but since 1974 it has been the home of Newark and Sherwood District Council.

NOTTINGHAMSHIRE — A1   79

St Wilfred, South Muskham ❸   1.5m N A46 ; 1m S B6325 ; 0.2m W

St Wilfred is a charming village church; the base of the west tower was built in the thirteenth century, but the rest of the building is up to two hundred years younger. It is typical of the local interpretation of the English Perpendicular style.

JUNCTIONS
Area north of Newark
B6325 Newark
A6075 Tuxford and Ollerton

Railway (London–Edinburgh) ❹   A46 to A6075 ; W then E

The railway which the A1 both crosses and runs alongside in this area is the main line connecting London with Doncaster, Leeds, York, Newcastle and Edinburgh.

High Marnham Power Station ❺   5.5m N B6325 ; 3.5m S A6075 ; 4m E

PowerGen's High Marnham generating station is just one of a number of large plants burning coal from the threatened Derbyshire, Nottinghamshire and Yorkshire coalfields.

Windmill, Tuxford ❻   1m N A6075 ; 1 m S A57 (east) ; 0.1m W

This is a tower mill, with a brick-built body and a wooden top which carried the sails. Unfortunately the sails have gone, but you can still see the small 'fantail', whose function was to turn the top of the mill in order to keep the sails pointing directly into the wind, and so achieve maximum efficiency.

Tower mills in various states of decay are visible at several places beside the A1. Windmills were used mainly either to grind corn into flour or to pump water for drainage.

A1 — NOTTINGHAMSHIRE

All Saints, Milton

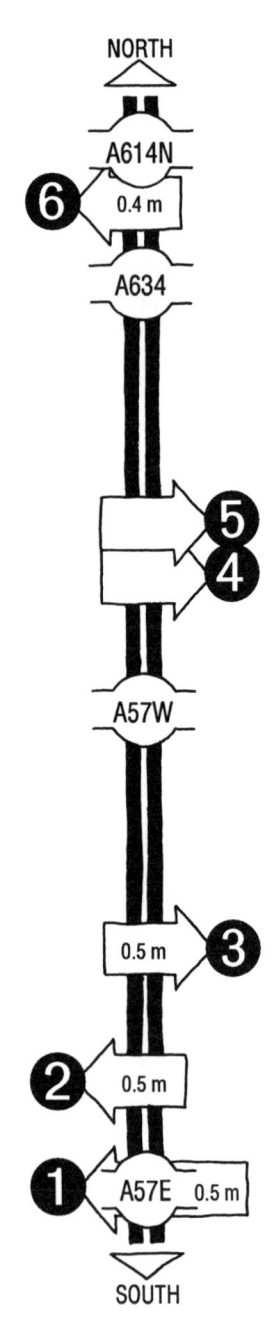

At A57 (east) ; 0.5m W

As you pass Markham Moor, with its fast food restaurants, take a look up the hill to the west. You will see a small white classical-style building with a low domed tower, looking strangely formal and out of place among the fields and hedgerows. This is All Saints' Church, in the village of Milton. It was built by the 4th Duke of Newcastle, in memory of his wife. He intended that it should be the parish church, but now it is unused and in the care of the Redundant Churches Fund. The architect was Robert Smirke, who was rather more famous for designing the British Museum and the Royal Mint.

Bevercotes colliery

1.25m N A57 (east) ; 4.25m S A57 (west) ; 0.5m W

British Coal East Pennine coalfield, Notts area coal measures. Named after Bevercotes, the village about a mile south of the mine. As this book goes to press, Bevercotes appears likely to close.

Gamston aerodrome

2.5m N A57 (east) ; 3m S A57 (west) ; 0.5m E

Gamston was planned as an operational bomber airfield, and opened as an RAF station in 1942. However, it was used mainly for training, and the RAF left a few years after the war. Many wartime reminders are left, including a hanger, several Nissen huts and the old control tower, which is now a private house. The airfield is still used by private and business aircraft.

Chesterfield Canal

1.5m N A57 (west) ; 3.5m S A634 ; adjacent E

Work on the Chesterfield canal was begun in 1771 by the famous engineer James Brindley and took five years to

NOTTINGHAMSHIRE — A1

complete. The tortuous bends you can see from the road are typical of Brindley's canals, which followed the contours of the land where later engineers would have constructed embankments and dug cuttings. The canal's purpose was to carry coal and iron from the Rother Valley to the River Trent and beyond. Mining subsidence and tunnel collapse have left the top section unnavigable, and leisure boats can now only travel as far as Worksop, about five miles away to the west.

The Barracks ⑤ 2m N A57 (west) ; 3m S A634 ; adj. E

Now a single private house, The Barracks was built around 1790. It stands at the foot of Barrack Hill, but we were unable to find out whether the hill was named after the house or vice versa. From the name, it seems obvious that soldiers were billeted here at some time, but surprisingly little seems to be known of the building's early history, and the current owner would like to find out more. So would we.

JUNCTIONS
Worksop area
A57 (east) Lincoln and A638 Retford
A57 (west) Worksop and A614 (south) Nottingham
A634 Blyth and Maltby (limited access)
A614 (north) Blyth and Bawtry

St Mary and St Martin, Blyth ⑥ 0.75m N A634 ; 0.5m S A614 ; 0.4m W

The Priory church of St Mary and St Martin stands out above the village, to the west of the A1. It is considered to be a supreme example of early Norman architecture. Building started in 1088 and was completed by 1100. It is a pity that someone in relatively modern times decided to use brick when replacing the wall on the end of the building which overlooks the road.

A1 — NOTTINGHAMSHIRE

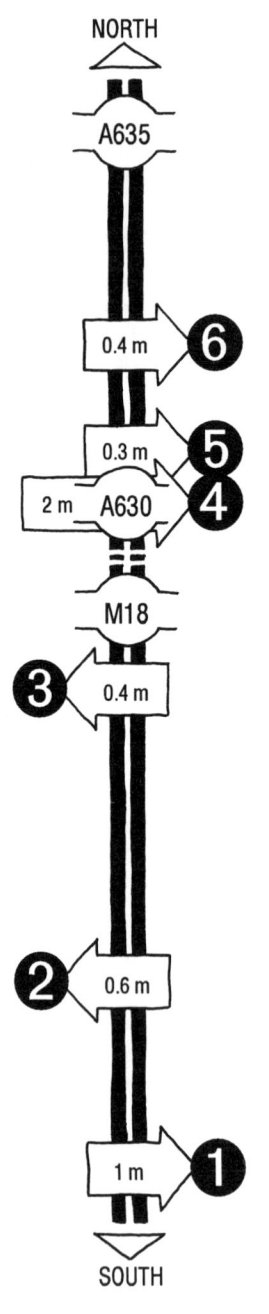

Harworth colliery ❶   1.75m N A614 ; 5.75m S M18 ; 1m E

British Coal, East Pennine coalfield, Notts area coal measures. At the time of writing, Harworth was one of the mines due to remain in operation.

Tickhill ❷   3.5m N A614 ; 4m S M18 ; 0.6m W

It is easy to dismiss Tickhill as just another nondescript village as you fly past on the A1(M). However, look a little closer and you will see the jelly-mould shape of the castle mound and the tower of the parish church, dedicated to St Mary the Virgin.

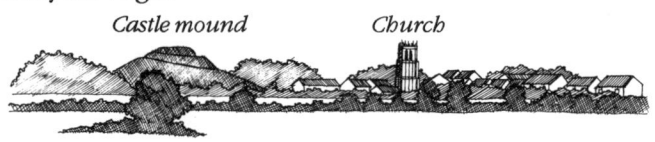

Castle mound   Church

Tickhill was a very important military and religious centre in Norman times. Most of the castle has gone, but there is still a good moat around the mound. The existing church is a classic in the English Perpendicular style, dating from about 1340. The tower carries several heraldic devices, including the arms of John of Gaunt.

St John, Wadworth ❸   6.75m N A614 ; 0.75m S M18 ; 0.4 W

Much of the Church of St John the Baptist at Wadworth dates from late-Norman times, so is now about 800 years old. The slender Perpendicular tower is only slightly more recent.

SOUTH YORKSHIRE — A1

Doncaster ④   At A630 ; 2m E

The skyline of Doncaster is dominated by the 170-ft (52-m) tower of St George's church. This was designed in the 1850s by Sir George Gilbert Scott, the Victorian master of blockbusters who is now remembered as much for St Pancras station as for anything else.

The A1 went through the centre of Doncaster until the bypass (the first section of the A1 to be built as motorway) was opened in 1961, and was the scene of some epic traffic jams at peak holiday times. The town has long been an important transport centre, being served in turn by Roman road, canals, coaching services and railways. The locomotive works here produced many famous steam engines, including the Flying Scotsman and Mallard.

JUNCTIONS

Doncaster area

M18
Hull and M1

A630
Doncaster and Rotherham

A635
Doncaster and Barnsley

Railway bridges, Doncaster ⑤   0.5m N A630 ; 2.75m S A635 ; 0.3m E

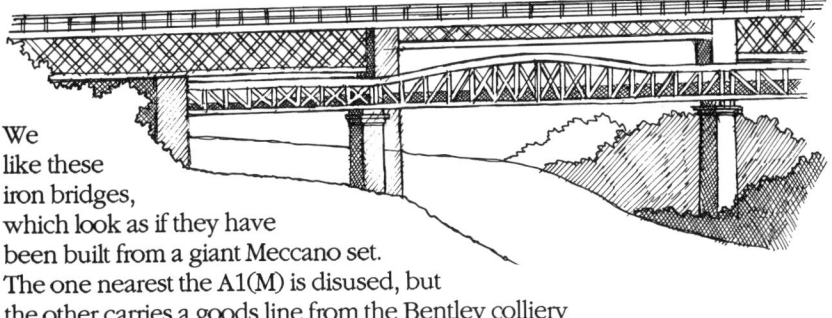

We like these iron bridges, which look as if they have been built from a giant Meccano set. The one nearest the A1(M) is disused, but the other carries a goods line from the Bentley colliery district. They span the the River Don Navigation, which connects Sheffield with the Humber.

Cusworth Hall ⑥   1.75m N A630 ; 2m S A635 ; 0.4m E

A stately home with an impressive view over the Don valley, Cusworth Hall is now a museum of South Yorkshire history. The house was rebuilt in 1740 by James Paine, who was much in demand at the time as a designer of homes for the Yorkshire gentry. The house at Nostell Priory, near Wakefield, is also one of his.

A1 — SOUTH YORKSHIRE

Robin Hood's Well ❶ 1.5m N A638 ; 1.5m S A639 ; adj. E

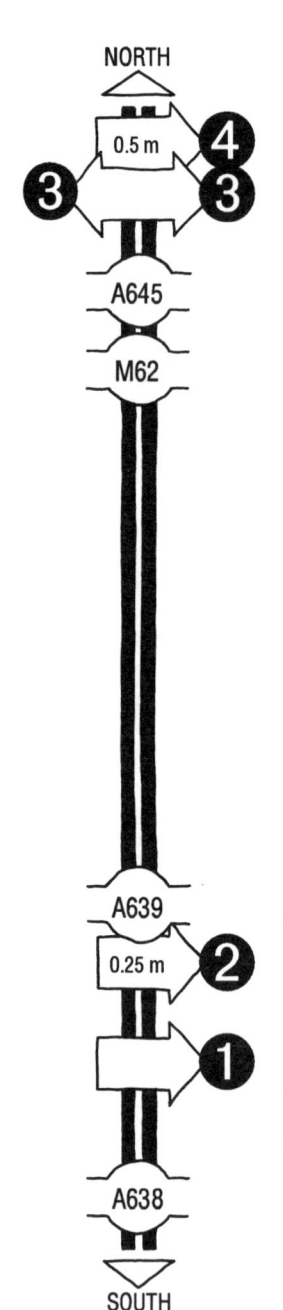

Robin Hood's Well was once outside the Robin Hood Inn, a coaching house at the centre of a village beside the Great North Road. The village has now gone, leaving just the small masonry building which once covered the well. It is believed that this was designed by Sir John Vanbrugh and erected in 1707. Vanbrugh usually exercised his talents on a rather grander scale, one of the most famous examples being the great house of Castle Howard, about 30 miles away to the north-east.

Robin Hood himself, nowadays often thought of as virtually a native of Nottingham, is believed to have dwelt in the forest of Barnsdale, which covered this area and joined up with Sherwood, many miles further south.

The well building was moved when the road was improved in the 1970s, and now stands looking rather lost beside a lay-by. It is used mainly as something to lean motorcycles against.

Summer House Farm ❷ 2.5m N A638 ; 0.5m S A639 ; 0.25m E

At first sight this looks like a small castle sitting on the ridge to the east of the road. However, the front is false, and the building is simply a farmhouse (see illustration opposite). Tradition has it that the house, originally called Barnsdale Summer House, was built for the mistress of a local squire, and rumours of an underground tunnel entrance permitting unobserved access still persist.

WEST YORKSHIRE — A1   85

River Aire; Aire and Calder Navigation ③
0.75m N A645; 0.5m S A162; crosses

This is part of an important network of waterways which connects industrial areas of Yorkshire, Derbyshire and Nottinghamshire with the North Sea, via the Humber estuary.

Literally millions of tonnes of coal, petroleum products, sand and gravel, limestone, steel and manufactured goods are shipped along this stretch of water.

Flour mills, Knottingley

River Aire

Flour mills, Knottingley ④
0.75m N A645; 0.5m S A162; 0.5m E

The large buildings beside the river (see illustration above) are flour mills belonging to Associated British Foods. They have recently been renovated and modernised.

Summer House Farm (see facing page)

JUNCTIONS
Barnsdale area
A638 Adwick-le-Street and Wakefield
A639 Pontefract (Barnsdale Bar)
M62 Trans-Pennine motorway linking Hull and Liverpool
A645 Knottingley and Pontefract

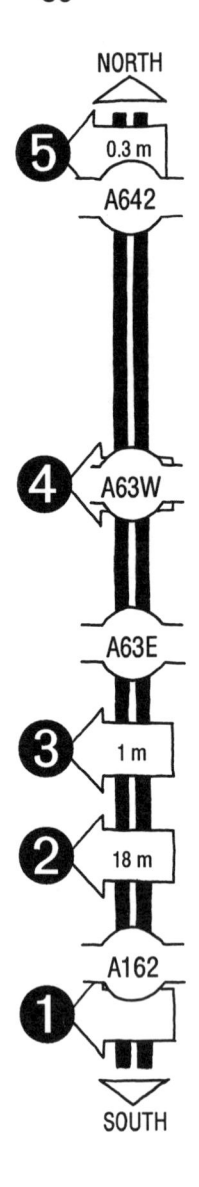

Ferrybridge Power Stations ①

1m N A645; 0.25m S A162; adjacent W

The power stations at Ferrybridge are visible from miles around. Ferrybridge 'C' was the first 2,000 megawatt station in Europe. It burns coal from nearby Kellingley colliery. This coal is delivered in barges, which are emptied by a unique 'tippler': this lifts them out of the water, hoists them 80 ft (25 m) into the air, and inverts them to dump 170 tonnes of coal each time!

In 1965, during a severe gale, the wind was amplified so much by the shape and positions of the cooling towers that it destroyed three of them. Since then, towers worldwide have been built with much thicker concrete skins.

Ferrybridge 'B' was opened in 1959 and closed in 1992. It has no cooling towers — it was able to draw enough cooling water directly from the adjacent River Aire.

TV mast, Emley Moor ②

1.25m N A162; 2m S A63 (east); 18m W

From the Fairburn area, the Emley Moor TV mast is prominent on a clear day, although it is 18 miles (29 km) away to the south-west. At 1084 ft (330 m), this is the tallest concrete structure in Britain. See the M1 (page 41) for further details.

Fairburn Ings Nature Reserve ③

2.25m N A162; 1m S A63 (east); 1m W

At first sight, the collection of lakes and wet meadowland which can be spotted to the west of the A1 looks like yet another area of useless industrial dereliction. However, it forms an important and long-established reserve managed by the Royal Society for the Protection of Birds (RSPB). The total of 240 different species which have been spotted here make it one of the best sites in England, and it is particularly rich in wildfowl and wading birds.

WEST YORKSHIRE — A1

The Boot and Shoe Inn ④ At A63 (west) ; adj. W

This pub stands at the junction of the road to Leeds, which lies about seven miles to the west. Here the Rockingham and Leeds Union post coaches turned off the Great North Road. It has been a famous landmark since the days of the turnpikes, when it marked the halfway point between Leeds and Selby.

JUNCTIONS
Castleford area
A162 Tadcaster
A63 (east) Selby
A63 (west) Leeds
A642 Garforth and Leeds

Almshouses, Aberford ⑤ 0.25m N A642 ; 2.5m S A64 ; 0.3m W

The Gascoigne Almshouses, built in 1844 in the gothic revival style. They became redundant as almshouses and were used by Leeds City Art Galleries as conservation workshops during the 1980s. The almshouses are unused at the time of writing, and they surely deserve a better fate than that.

A1 — WEST YORKSHIRE

Bowcliffe Hall ❶   1.5m N A64 ; 2.5m S A659 ; 0.1m W

Glimpses of Bowcliffe Hall can just be seen to the west of the A1; the prominent buildings overlooking the carriageway are only outbuildings. A handsome and extensive mid-Georgian house, the Hall is now the head office of Bayford Energy plc.

St Luke, St Edward, Clifford ❷   2.5m N A64 ; 1.5m S A659 ; 0.5m and 0.75m E

St Luke's

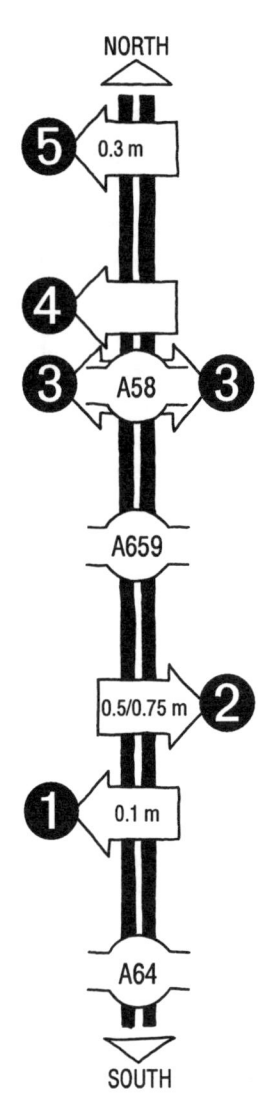

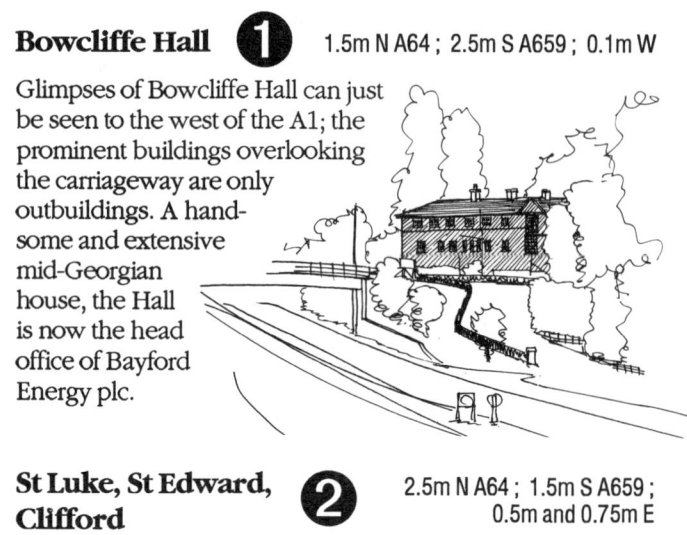

The small mediaeval church with the square tower, near the A1, is St Luke's, the parish church of Clifford — a pleasant building, but not exceptional.

More interesting is St Edward's, the Roman Catholic church on the other side of the village. It was built in Victorian times through the initiative of a Mrs Grimston, whose husband was a local mill owner, and Father Clifford, the first priest. These two spread their net very widely when it came to raising building funds, and such notables as the King of Sardinia, the Queen of France and the Pope himself were persuaded to put their hands into their pockets.

The church was built to the design of a young Scot who incorporated various features from continental churches into what he considered an ideal design.

St Edward's

NORTH YORKSHIRE — A1

River Wharfe ③
At A58; crosses

Beside Wetherby the A1 crosses the Wharfe. This is one of the many Yorkshire rivers which flow eastwards from the Pennines to enter the North Sea via the Ouse system and the Humber estuary.

Between here and Scotch Corner the road also crosses the Nidd, the Ure and the Swale.

Wetherby ④
A58 to 1.5m N A58; adjacent W

Wetherby is a market town which stands at the halfway point between London and Edinburgh. It is at the start of the Vale of York, the broad fertile valley between the Yorkshire Dales to the west and the Hambleton Hills to the east.

JUNCTIONS
Wetherby area
A64 Leeds and York
A659 Tadcaster and Otley
A58 Wetherby and Leeds

Wetherby racecourse

The A1 passes between the town and Wetherby racecourse, which is devoted exclusively to National Hunt racing. The racecourse is about one and a half miles around. Fortunately, the National Hunt season runs from autumn to spring, so race traffic does not clash with heavy summer-holiday traffic.

All Saints, Kirk Deighton ⑤
2.25m N A58; 5.75 S A59; 0.3m W

All Saints is a twelfth-century church, restored in 1875. As you approach from the south, it is difficult to tell which side of the road it is on.

A1 — NORTH YORKSHIRE

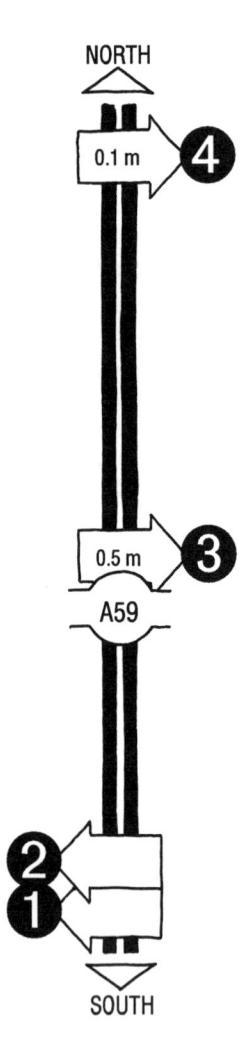

Lodge, Ribstone Hall ①

4.25m N A58 ; 2.75m S A 59 ; adjacent W

Look out for the driveway entrance to Ribstone Hall standing beside a now by-passed fragment of the old carriageway. There is a fine small lodge, and gateposts guarded by stone lions.

The Hall lies in parkland about 1.5 miles away to the west. It was built in 1674 for Sir Henry Goodricke, a colourful seventeenth-century diplomat. He was sent to the court of Madrid by Charles II as an envoy extraordinary to act as a mediator in the war between France and Spain, but was thrown out because the Spanish disliked Charles' foreign policies. He was MP for Boroughbridge from 1689 until his death in 1705.

The Bridge Inn ②

4.5m N A58 ; 2.5m S A59 ; adj. W

This used to be a small inn serving the needs of casual travellers on the Great North Road, but it has developed considerably since those days. The A1 now passes what was the back of the original inn, and a section of the old Great North Road acts as a service road on the other side.

NORTH YORKSHIRE — A1

Allerton Park ③ 0.5m N A59 ; 5m S A6055 ; 0.5m E

JUNCTIONS
Knares-borough area
A59 Knaresborough and York

Allerton Park is a splendid Victorian Gothic mansion which was mainly constructed in 1845–51, but retaining some parts of a house originally built by the Duke of York in the late 1780s. Open to the public from May to October, it is also the home of a curious restaurant called 'The Bunker', which has the Second World War as its theme.

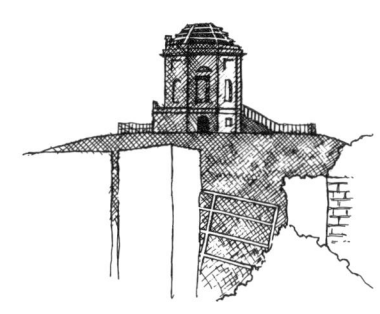

The small domed 'Temple of Victory' which is clearly visible in the park dates from the time of an earlier house, c. 1780. This is a fine piece of Georgian landscape adornment which has unfortunately become derelict.

Ornham's Hall ④ 4.25m N A59 ; 1.25m S A6055 ; 0.1m E

Ornham's Hall is visible about two miles south of Boroughbridge. Designed in 1835 by John Buonarotti Papworth, a celebrated architect most famous for his work at Cheltenham Spa, it is a nicely proportioned 'gentleman's house' of the period, but otherwise unremarkable.

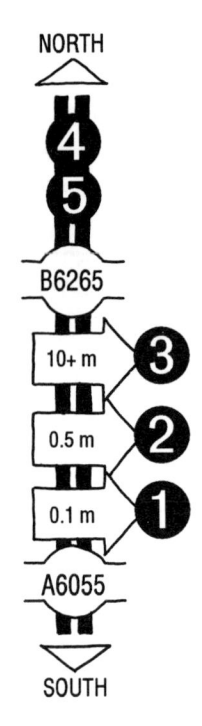

The Devil's Arrows

0.5m N A6055 ; 1.75m S B6265 ; 0.1m E

In the fields between the road and the town you can see three large standing stones or monoliths, each approximately 20 ft (6 m) high. These are the Devil's Arrows. They lie on a north–south line stretching 570 ft (175 m). It is believed that there were originally at least five stones in the alignment.

Tradition has it that they fell from the Devil's rope when he tried to hang his grandmother, but we are a little sceptical about this. The explanation that they are the remnants of a Bronze Age religious centre seems more plausible. The nearest source of this type of stone is Knaresborough, over six miles away, and it is interesting to try to imagine how these were dragged here, since we estimate each one must weigh about forty tonnes.

Boroughbridge

0.75m N A6055 ; 1.5m S B6265 ; 0.5m E

In the heyday of coaching (about 1790–1835), Boroughbridge was one of the busiest towns on the Great North Road. The Crown Inn kept more than a hundred horses stabled in its yard, and coaches with such romantic names as The Hero, The Highflyer, The North Star and The North Briton changed their teams here.

The buildings with distinctively-shaped roofs are part of Warwick and Co's Anchor Brewery and Maltings. Although this appears to be in Boroughbridge, it is really in Langthorpe, just across the River Ure from the town. The conical structure is on top of the oldest maltings in Yorkshire, built around 1850, while the towers are only slightly newer. Sadly, barley is no longer malted here, and the whole brewery complex was semi-derelict when we visited it in 1991.

NORTH YORKSHIRE — A1

Boroughbridge

JUNCTIONS

Boroughbridge area

A6055
Boroughbridge and Knaresborough

B6265
Boroughbridge and Ripon

The Hambleton Hills ③   A6055 to A684 ; 10+m E

If the weather is good as you pass through this area, you will see the Hambleton Hills ten miles or so away to the east. The hills rise about 1200 ft (350 m). If conditions are really good, you will be able to spot the White Horse of Kilburn at the southern end of the range. This was cut into the limestone hillside in 1857. It was the brainchild of local schoolmasters John Hodgson and Thomas Taylor, who were impressed by the ancient figures inscribed on the chalk downlands of Southern England. Taylor's schoolboys did most of the digging, eventually producing this horse, 312 ft (95 m) long and 226 ft (69 m) high.

The headquarters of the famous Yorkshire Gliding Club at Sutton Bank is just a little to the north of the White Horse.

Dere Street ④   0.75m N B6265 to A66 (Scotch Corner)

Dere Street was the Roman road running from York northwards to Corbridge and Hadrian's Wall. Typical of Roman highway engineering, it runs dead straight for long stretches and provides an easy route for the A1 up the Vale of York and beyond.

Leeming Lane ⑤   0.75m N B6265 to 2m S A684

Nowadays the stretch of road from Kirkby Hill, just north of Boroughbridge, to Leeming tends to be rather undistinguished. Boring would be a good word for it. However, you are motoring over Leeming Lane, which a hundred or so years ago was famous far beyond Yorkshire for its unofficial horse races. Fortunes were won and lost on this thirteen-mile length.

A1 — NORTH YORKSHIRE

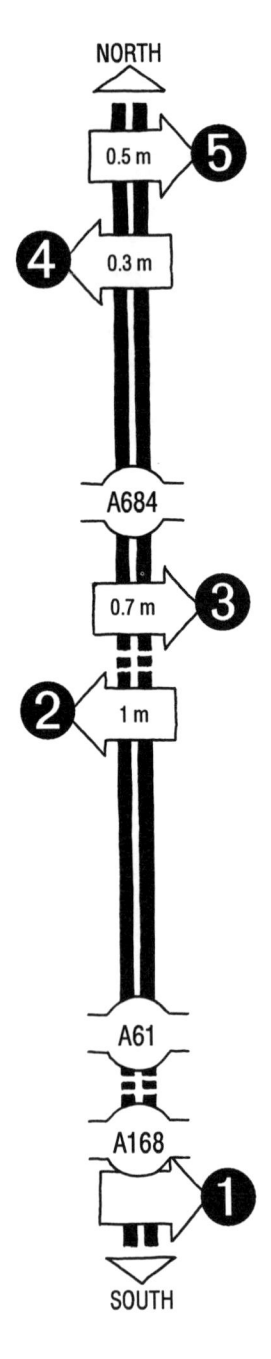

Dishforth airfield ❶   1.25m N B6265; 1m S A168; adj. E

Dishforth was opened in 1936 as a bomber station for the RAF: in those days even bombers used to take off and land on grass. The runways were built in 1943 to cope with four-engined aircraft, mainly Halifaxes. The one which runs parallel with the A1 is just over a mile long.

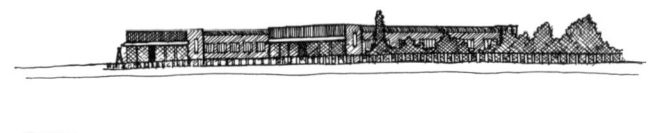

No warplanes are currently based at Dishforth, but on weekdays you may see trainers (Jet Provosts and Bulldogs at the time of writing) making practice landings here. At weekends it is a centre of gliding activity.

Camp Hill ❷   4.5m N A61; 4.75m S A684; 1m W

A classic early-nineteenth century mansion, owned and originally occupied by the Sergeantson family. It is just visible through the trees of its fifty-acre wooded park.

Control tower, Leeming airfield ❸   8m N A61; 1.25m S A684; 0.7m E

Leeming started as a flying club in 1938, but was soon taken over for the RAF. Runways were built, and the airfield opened for action in the summer of 1940, the base for squadrons of night fighters and bombers. At first, most of the aircraft here were Halifaxes, but towards the end of the war a number of Lancaster squadrons operated from Leeming. Since then, it has been the home of a wide variety of RAF training operations, using many different types of aircraft.

NORTH YORKSHIRE — A1

Leeming control tower

Leeming was closed for a period in the mid-1980s for re-development as a Tornado base. Extensive 'hard' shelters for the aircraft were built at that time. As you are driven by on the A1, you can often see Tornados coming in to land with their wings in the 'swung-out' position for low-speed operation.

JUNCTIONS
Ripon/ North- allerton area
A168 Thirsk
A61 Ripon and Thirsk
A684 Northallerton and Wensleydale, and eventually Kendal

Street House ④ 3m N A684 ; 2.75m S A6136 (south) ; 0.3m W

Street House is a very interesting early-Georgian brick house. The plan is quite original, in that the centre portion projects to the front and back in the form of an octagon.

Killerby Hall ⑤ 4.5m N A684 ; 1.25m S A6136 (south) ; 0.5m E

This appears to have been the property and residence of the Booth family, who were the principal landowners in the area, until the end of the nineteenth century. The hall stands on the site of a fortified manor built around 1300 by Sir Brian Fitz Allen, the Earl of Arundel.

A1 — NORTH YORKSHIRE

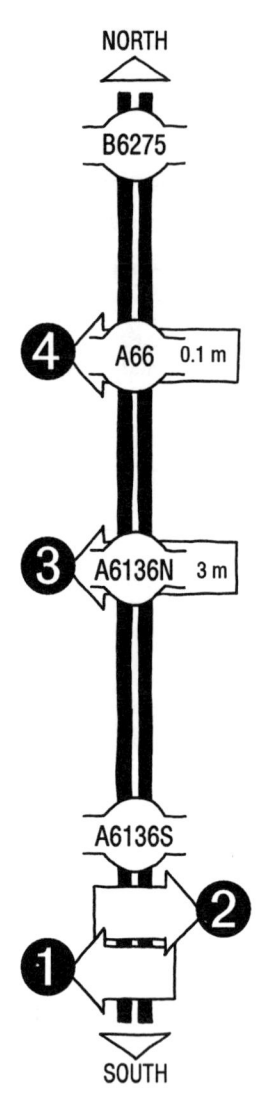

Yorkshire Dales ①
Visible to the west

All along this section of the A1, the hills at the start of the Yorkshire Dales are visible a few miles to the west. These rise to over 2,000 ft (600 m). Always beautiful, the Dales gained extra fame in the 1980s as the setting of James Herriot's books and TV series about life as a country vet.

Catterick airfield ②
5m N A684 ; 0.7m S A6136 (south) ; adj. E

This is one of Britain's oldest permanent airfields, having been opened in 1914 for the Royal Flying Corps, the forerunner of the RAF. It has been the home of many legendary fighter aircraft, including Sopwith Pups from the First World War, and Hurricanes and Spitfires from the Second.

In 1945 Catterick became the headquarters of the RAF Regiment, which is still based there. Although much of the training is centred around ground combat and firefighting, the airfield remains operative for light communications aircraft and gliders.

Catterick Garrison is a military town a couple of miles to the west of the A1. It is remembered without much affection by a generation of National Service conscripts as the place where they endured their basic training.

Richmond ③
At A6136 (north) ; 3m W

Richmond is an attractive ancient town to the west of the A1 and north of Catterick Garrison (see above). The most obvious building is the light-coloured stone barracks on the hillside overlooking the town. Once the headquarters of the Green Howards regiment, the barracks have recently been converted into private housing.

Lower down the valley is the massive keep of Richmond Castle. This dates from about 1170, although other parts of the castle were built a hundred years earlier, shortly after the

NORTH YORKSHIRE — A1

Richmond Castle keep

Norman conquest. From the road, the keep seems to stand on its own just south of the town, and can be quite tricky to see.

Richmond is at the start of Swaledale, one of the most beautiful of the Yorkshire Dales, and famous for its hardy sheep. You cross the river Swale on the A1 just north of Catterick.

Scotch Corner Hotel ❹   At A66 ; 0.1m W

> **JUNCTIONS**
>
> **Richmond area**
> **A6136 (south)**
> Catterick and Richmond
>
> **A6136 (north)**
> Catterick
>
> **A66**
> Stainmore and
> **A6108** Richmond
> (Scotch Corner)
>
> **B6275**
> Piercebridge. The junction at which, going north, the A1 becomes the A1(M) again.

The Scotch Corner Hotel was built in the 1930s, but the junction at which it stands has been important since Roman times. Here the A66, the Bowes Moor Road, branches off to the left to climb up over the Pennines through Stainmore Gap (a notorious winter snow blockage point) and on to Penrith and Carlisle. This was one of the few Roman trans-Pennine routes and the main supply road to the western end of Hadrian's Wall. The A1 swings to the north-east here, having followed Roman Dere Street since Boroughbridge (see also page 93).

In the coaching days, the London to Glasgow coaches turned left here while the Edinburgh ones continued straight on up the Great North Road. Nowadays the main London–Glasgow route follows the M6 instead.

A1 — COUNTY DURHAM

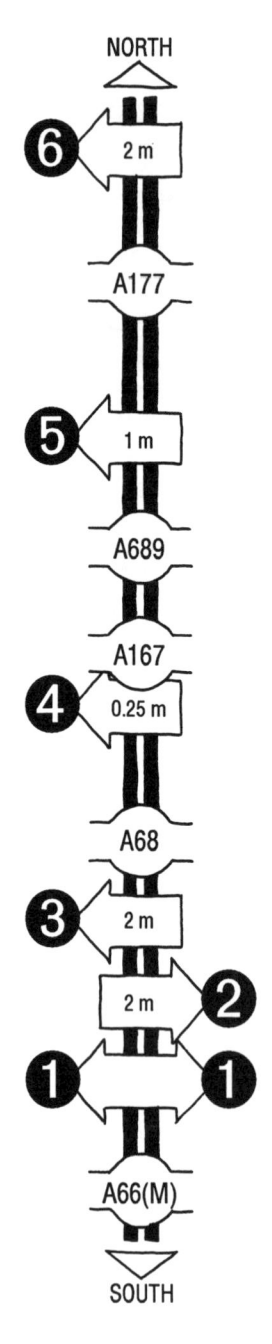

River Tees ❶ 1.5m N A66(M) ; 3m S A68 ; crosses

The A1(M) crosses the river Tees about seven miles north of Scotch Corner. At this point the river gives little indication of the industrial waterway it will become as it flows past Middlesbrough, only a dozen miles to the east.

Darlington ❷ A66(M) to A68 ; 2m E

The 'cradle of the railways'. A small Saxon settlement which grew into a prosperous Norman market town. Much later it became a railway-related industrial centre, mainly because Edward Pease, a local businessman, sponsored and aided George Stephenson in the development of the Stockton and Darlington Railway. This was the line on which the first-ever passenger train ran on 27 September 1825, pulled by the steam engine Active, later renamed the Locomotion, which is preserved in the Darlington Railway Centre.

Walworth Castle ❸ 3.5m N A66(M) ; 1m S A68 ; 2m W

Walworth Castle has overlooked the route of the Great North Road for 800 years, yet remarkably little is written about it. It is believed to have been built in 1189 for one Gilbert Hansard. His descendants conducted their lives in the robust manner typical of the age, including being very active in putting down the Peasants' Revolt of 1381.

The castle fell into decay and was repaired and rebuilt at various times during its life. It seems to be distinguished mainly because James VI of Scotland stayed overnight here in April 1603 when he was making his way south to London for his coronation as King of England.

Walworth Castle was last used as a private dwelling in 1935. Since then it has served as an Officers' Mess for the Durham Light Infantry, a prisoner-of-war camp, and a girls' school. Now it is a hotel offering rooms with four-poster beds. Also, in our experience, the bar meals are excellent.

COUNTY DURHAM — A1

Fujitsu factory ④   2m N A68 ; 0.5m S A167 ; 0.25m W

A new electronics plant belonging to Fujitsu Microelectronics, the world's second-largest computer company. The factory cost £400 million and was opened in mid-1991.

With this Fujitsu plant, the nearby Nissan car factory and numerous smaller operations, the North-east of England now has the largest concentration of Japanese industry outside Japan.

Lime works, Ferryhill ⑤   2m N A689 ; 4m S A177 ; 1m W

Operated by Steetley Quarry Products, this plant takes raw material from local quarries. There are many worked-out limestone quarries in this area.

Durham ⑥   3m N A177 ; 1.75m S A690 ; 2m W

Once one of the most important Christian centres in Europe, Durham is dominated by the cathedral, which is dedicated to St Cuthbert, a seventh-century teacher, bishop and monk. Invading Danes would not allow him to rest in peace in his original tomb on Lindisfarne, so his remains were eventually brought to this settlement beside the River Wear in 999. The place became a shrine and the town soon began to thrive. The existing castle and cathedral date from the eleventh century. Throughout the Middle Ages, the Prince Bishops of Durham were immensely powerful.

JUNCTIONS

Darlington/ Durham area

A66(M)
Darlington and Teeside (limited access)

A68
Darlington and Bishop Auckland

A167
Darlington and Newton Aycliffe

A689
Bishop Auckland and Hartlepool

A177
Durham

A1 — COUNTY DURHAM

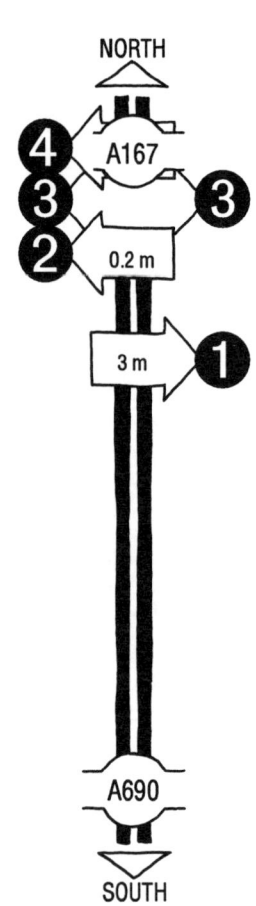

Durham cathedral The central tower of the cathedral is the most prominent landmark in the town. It is 218 ft (66 m) high. The cathedral was built between 1093 and 1133, in the Romanesque style, of which it is one of the finest examples.

Durham Castle The castle is a hexagonal building just north of the cathedral. As it is a little lower, it is much harder to spot from the road. It was built a few years before the cathedral and was under the control of the Prince Bishops of Durham for hundreds of years. In 1640, during the English Civil War, the castle was badly damaged. However, unlike many of the others, it was rebuilt rather than left as a ruin, and now serves as a hall of residence for the University of Durham.

Unfortunately Durham Castle was not built on such solid rock as the cathedral, and although it is still one of the most complete Norman castles in Britain it now requires expensive repairs if it is to stand for future centuries.

Penshaw Monument   4m N A690; 2m S A167; 3m E

The Greek temple on top of Penshaw Hill dominates the view to the east of Chester-le-Street. This is a monument to 'Radical Jack' Lambton, who died in 1840. He was a great Liberal politician who became Governor-General of Canada and was made the first Earl of Durham. The monument was funded by public subscription and completed in 1844. It is a fairly close copy of the Temple of Theseus in Athens.

COUNTY DURHAM — A1

Lumley Castle ②   5m N A690 ; 1m S A167 ; 0.2m W

On the site of a manor house, the castle was built by Sir Ralph Lumley in 1392, after he had obtained a licence from both the Bishop of Durham and the King. The battlements on a building are called crenellations, and Lumley had to get a licence to crenellate before he could construct a fortified building. Ralph Lumley was killed during the battle of Cirencester in 1400, while fighting for the Earl of Kent in a rebellion of former dukes.

JUNCTIONS
Durham/ Chester- le-Street area
A690 Durham and Sunderland
A167 Chester-le-Street and **A693** Stanley and **A183** Sunderland

The castle did not change much for several centuries, until it was 'modernised' around 1720 by Vanbrugh for the second Earl of Scarborough. It was again refurbished at the turn of the twentieth century, and briefly served as a rather glamorous hall of residence for Durham University. Now it is a hotel and conference centre, offering four-poster beds and Elizabethan banquets.

River Wear ③   5.75m N A690 ; 0.25m S A167 ; crosses

Chester-le-Street ④   At A167 ; adjacent W

The monks of Lindisfarne came here in AD 883 with the body of St Cuthbert, and established a church on the site of a Roman camp. St Cuthbert's mortal remains were moved on to Durham a century later, but the present church of St Mary and St Cuthbert is on that same site, and its splendid 189ft (57m) spire is clearly visible from the A1(M). From 883 to 995 Chester-le-Street was the seat of the Bishops of Lindisfarne.

A complete contrast to the church is provided by the steel-and-plastic arched roof of the modern Council offices.

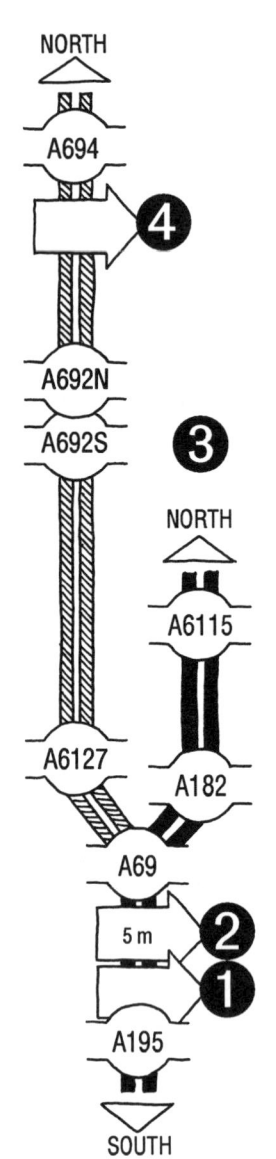

Washington ①
A195 to A182 ; adjacent E

This is the place which lent its name to the capital of the USA because of its connections with the first President, George Washington.

Washington was a mining village which had some of the oldest active pits in the country. However, with the introduction of the Clean Air acts, and the wind-down of industry after the 1939–45 war, came a decline in the demand for coal. Revival was needed, and so a new town was proposed in 1964 in an attempt to attract new industries to the area. In 1967 Washington was reborn as Washington New Town. Since then, growth has been good in a wide variety of industries; the biggest employer is now the Nissan car company, which has built a vast plant nearby. The New Town takes the form of a series of villages, planned to cover the remains of collieries and other derelict sites.

Washington Old Hall is in the heart of the town. This was the home of five generations of George Washington's ancestors, including his grandfather. By the early 1950s the building had become sadly neglected and was virtually derelict, awaiting demolition. Fortunately the local people rallied round and restored the Hall before presenting it to the National Trust. It is now a popular attraction, particularly with visitors from the USA. On American public holidays you may spot the Stars and Stripes flying here — a clear reminder of the transatlantic tie.

Wearside ②
A195 to A182 ; 5m E

From this stretch of road there are good views down to Sunderland and the old shipbuilding yards of Wearside.

Tyneside ③

The A1 curves round to the east, to cross the Tyne between Gateshead and Newcastle. However, through traffic now follows a new route around the west of the Tyneside towns to rejoin the A1 further north. This route follows the new A69 and crosses the river near Blaydon, which gave its name to the song Blaydon Races, the popular Geordie anthem.

TYNE & WEAR — A1

Tyneside was once one of the most vigorous industrial centres in the world — famous for shipbuilding and heavy engineering. Much of this industry has now gone, but new industries are encouraged to develop here and the area is still a very important business centre.

MetroCentre ④ 1.5m N A692 (north) ; 0.75m S A694 ; adj. E

The MetroCentre is a huge shopping and leisure complex beside the new main road. On the single site there are over 300 shops and 50 eating-places, as well as an indoor fairground, a 10-screen cinema and a large tenpin-bowling alley.

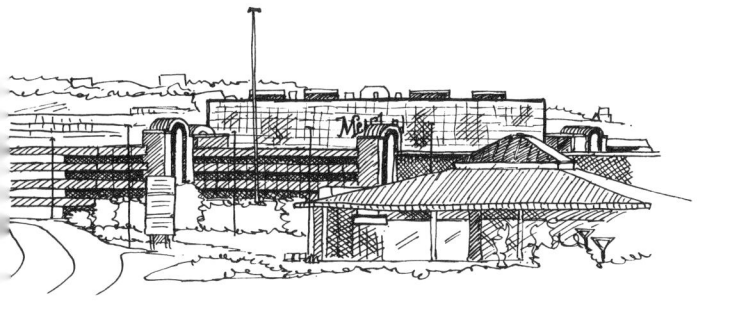

No doubt many visitors will be surprised to discover that this very American-style attraction is owned by the English Church Commissioners.

On to Scotland

The A1 continues north through the Border country into Scotland. It keeps close to the east coast before swinging west beside the Firth of Forth and on to its end at Edinburgh. Although still a trunk road, there are no sections of motorway standard, and so it falls outside the scope of this book.

JUNCTIONS

Washington/ Tyneside area

A195
Washington

A69
Blaydon (see also junction information below)

A182
Washington

A6115
Gateshead and
A194 South Shields; the end of the A1(M).

A69 JUNCTIONS

A6127
Birtley and Gateshead

A692 (south)
Consett

A692 (north)
Gateshead and Newcastle

A694
Consett